Singapore MATH PRACTICE

Appropriate for Students in GRADE 5

Frank Schaffer
An imprint of Carson-Dellosa Publishing LLC
Greensboro, North Carolina

ISBN 978-0-7682-3994-2
245107784

INTRODUCTION TO SINGAPORE MATH

Welcome to Singapore Math! The math curriculum in Singapore has been recognized worldwide for its excellence in producing students highly skilled in mathematics. Students in Singapore have ranked at the top in the world in mathematics on the *Trends in International Mathematics and Science Study* (TIMSS) in 1993, 1995, 2003, and 2008. Because of this, Singapore Math has gained in interest and popularity in the United States.

Singapore Math curriculum aims to help students develop the necessary math concepts and process skills for everyday life and to provide students with the ability to formulate, apply, and solve problems. Mathematics in the Singapore Primary (Elementary) Curriculum cover fewer topics but in greater depth. Key math concepts are introduced and built-on to reinforce various mathematical ideas and thinking. Students in Singapore are typically one grade level ahead of students in the United States.

The following pages provide examples of the various math problem types and skill sets taught in Singapore.

At an elementary level, some simple mathematical skills can help students understand mathematical principles. These skills are the counting-on, counting-back, and crossing-out methods. Note that these methods are most useful when the numbers are small.

1. The Counting-On Method

Used for addition of two numbers. Count on in 1s with the help of a picture or number line.

$$7 + 4 = \textbf{11}$$

2. The Counting-Back Method

Used for subtraction of two numbers. Count back in 1s with the help of a picture or number line.

$$16 - 3 = \textbf{13}$$

3. The Crossing-Out Method

Used for subtraction of two numbers. Cross out the number of items to be taken away. Count the remaining ones to find the answer.

$$20 - 12 = \textbf{8}$$

A **number bond** shows the relationship in a simple addition or subtraction problem. The number bond is based on the concept "part-part-whole." This concept is useful in teaching simple addition and subtraction to young children.

To find a whole, students must add the two parts.
To find a part, students must subtract the other part from the whole.

The different types of number bonds are illustrated below.

1. Number Bond (single digits)

3 (part) + 6 (part) = **9** (whole)

9 (whole) − 3 (part) = **6** (part)

9 (whole) − 6 (part) = **3** (part)

2. Addition Number Bond (single digits)

= 9 + 1 + 4   Make a ten first.

= 10 + 4

= **14**

3. Addition Number Bond (double and single digits)

= 2 + 5 + 10   Regroup 15 into 5 and 10.

= 7 + 10

= **17**

4. Subtraction Number Bond (double and single digits)

10 − 7 = 3

3 + 2 = **5**

5. Subtraction Number Bond (double digits)

10 − 5 = 5

10 − 10 = 0

5 + 0 = **5**

Students should understand that multiplication is repeated addition and that division is the grouping of all items into equal sets.

1. Repeated Addition (Multiplication)

Mackenzie eats 2 rolls a day. How many rolls does she eat in 5 days?

$$2 + 2 + 2 + 2 + 2 = 10$$
$$5 \times 2 = 10$$

She eats **10** rolls in 5 days.

2. The Grouping Method (Division)

Mrs. Lee makes 14 sandwiches. She gives all the sandwiches equally to 7 friends. How many sandwiches does each friend receive?

$$14 \div 7 = 2$$

Each friend receives **2** sandwiches.

One of the basic but essential math skills students should acquire is to perform the 4 operations of whole numbers and fractions. Each of these methods is illustrated below.

1. The Adding-Without-Regrouping Method

```
  H  T  O
  3  2  1        O: Ones
+ 5  6  8        T: Tens
---------
  8  8  9        H: Hundreds
```

Since no regrouping is required, add the digits in each place value accordingly.

2. The Adding-by-Regrouping Method

```
   H  T  O
  ¹4  9  2       O: Ones
+  1  5  3       T: Tens
----------
   6  4  5       H: Hundreds
```

In this example, regroup 14 tens into 1 hundred 4 tens.

3. The Adding-by-Regrouping-Twice Method

```
    H T O
   ¹2 ¹8 6
  +  3 6 5
  ─────────
     6 5 1
```

O: Ones
T: Tens
H: Hundreds

Regroup twice in this example.
First, regroup 11 ones into 1 ten 1 one.
Second, regroup 15 tens into 1 hundred 5 tens.

4. The Subtracting-Without-Regrouping Method

```
    H T O
    7 3 9
  - 3 2 5
  ─────────
    4 1 4
```

O: Ones
T: Tens
H: Hundreds

Since no regrouping is required, subtract the digits in each place value accordingly.

5. The Subtracting-by-Regrouping Method

```
    H T O
    5 ⁷8 ¹¹1
  - 2 4 7
  ─────────
    3 3 4
```

O: Ones
T: Tens
H: Hundreds

In this example, students cannot subtract 7 ones from 1 one. So, regroup the tens and ones. Regroup 8 tens 1 one into 7 tens 11 ones.

6. The Subtracting-by-Regrouping-Twice Method

```
    H T O
   ⁷8 ⁹0 ¹⁰0
  -  5 9 3
  ─────────
     2 0 7
```

O: Ones
T: Tens
H: Hundreds

In this example, students cannot subtract 3 ones from 0 ones and 9 tens from 0 tens. So, regroup the hundreds, tens, and ones. Regroup 8 hundreds into 7 hundreds 9 tens 10 ones.

7. The Multiplying-Without-Regrouping Method

```
      T O
      2 4
    ×   2
  ─────────
      4 8
```

O: Ones
T: Tens

Since no regrouping is required, multiply the digit in each place value by the multiplier accordingly.

8. The Multiplying-With-Regrouping Method

```
     H T O
    ¹3 ²4 9
  ×      3
  ─────────
   1, 0 4 7
```

O: Ones
T: Tens
H: Hundreds

In this example, regroup 27 ones into 2 tens 7 ones, and 14 tens into 1 hundred 4 tens.

9. The Dividing-Without-Regrouping Method

```
        2 4 1
      ─────────
    2 ) 4 8 2
       -4
       ───
        8
       -8
       ───
          2
         -2
         ───
          0
```

Since no regrouping is required, divide the digit in each place value by the divisor accordingly.

10. The Dividing-With-Regrouping Method

```
        1 6 6
      ─────────
    5 ) 8 3 0
       -5
       ───
        3 3
       -3 0
       ─────
          3 0
         -3 0
         ─────
            0
```

In this example, regroup 3 hundreds into 30 tens and add 3 tens to make 33 tens. Regroup 3 tens into 30 ones.

11. The Addition-of-Fractions Method

$$\frac{1}{6} \times \frac{2}{2} + \frac{1}{4} \times \frac{3}{3} = \frac{2}{12} + \frac{3}{12} = \frac{5}{12}$$

Always remember to make the denominators common before adding the fractions.

12. The Subtraction-of-Fractions Method

$$\frac{1}{2} \times \frac{5}{5} - \frac{1}{5} \times \frac{2}{2} = \frac{5}{10} - \frac{2}{10} = \frac{3}{10}$$

Always remembers to make the denominators common before subtracting the fractions.

13. The Multiplication-of-Fractions Method

$$\frac{\cancel{3}^1}{5} \times \frac{1}{\cancel{9}_3} = \frac{1}{15}$$

When the numerator and the denominator have a common multiple, reduce them to their lowest fractions.

14. The Division-of-Fractions Method

$$\frac{7}{9} \div \frac{1}{6} = \frac{7}{\cancel{9}_3} \times \frac{\cancel{6}^2}{1} = \frac{14}{3} = 4\frac{2}{3}$$

When dividing fractions, first change the division sign (÷) to the multiplication sign (×). Then, switch the numerator and denominator of the fraction on the right hand side. Multiply the fractions in the usual way.

Model drawing is an effective strategy used to solve math word problems. It is a visual representation of the information in word problems using bar units. By drawing the models, students will know of the variables given in the problem, the variables to find, and even the methods used to solve the problem.

Drawing models is also a versatile strategy. It can be applied to simple word problems involving addition, subtraction, multiplication, and division. It can also be applied to word problems related to fractions, decimals, percentage, and ratio.

The use of models also trains students to think in an algebraic manner, which uses symbols for representation.

The different types of bar models used to solve word problems are illustrated below.

1. The model that involves addition

Melissa has 50 blue beads and 20 red beads. How many beads does she have altogether?

$50 + 20 = \mathbf{70}$

2. The model that involves subtraction

Ben and Andy have 90 toy cars. Andy has 60 toy cars. How many toy cars does Ben have?

$90 - 60 = \mathbf{30}$

3. The model that involves comparison

Mr. Simons has 150 magazines and 110 books in his study. How many more magazines than books does he have?

$150 - 110 = \mathbf{40}$

4. The model that involves two items with a difference

A pair of shoes costs $109. A leather bag costs $241 more than the pair of shoes. How much is the leather bag?

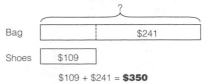

$109 + 241 = \mathbf{\$350}$

5. The model that involves multiples

Mrs. Drew buys 12 apples. She buys 3 times as many oranges as apples. She also buys 3 times as many cherries as oranges. How many pieces of fruit does she buy altogether?

$13 \times 12 = \textbf{156}$

6. The model that involves multiples and difference

There are 15 students in Class A. There are 5 more students in Class B than in Class A. There are 3 times as many students in Class C than in Class A. How many students are there altogether in the three classes?

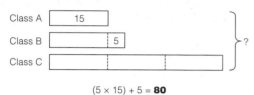

$(5 \times 15) + 5 = \textbf{80}$

7. The model that involves creating a whole

Ellen, Giselle, and Brenda bake 111 muffins. Giselle bakes twice as many muffins as Brenda. Ellen bakes 9 fewer muffins than Giselle. How many muffins does Ellen bake?

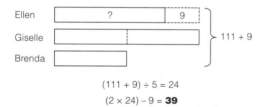

$(111 + 9) \div 5 = 24$

$(2 \times 24) - 9 = \textbf{39}$

8. The model that involves sharing

There are 183 tennis balls in Basket A and 97 tennis balls in Basket B. How many tennis balls must be transferred from Basket A to Basket B so that both baskets contain the same number of tennis balls?

$183 - 97 = 86$

$86 \div 2 = \textbf{43}$

9. The model that involves fractions

George had 355 marbles. He lost $\frac{1}{5}$ of the marbles and gave $\frac{1}{4}$ of the remaining marbles to his brother. How many marbles did he have left?

L: Lost
B: Brother
R: Remaining

5 parts → 355 marbles

1 part → $355 \div 5 = 71$ marbles

3 parts → $3 \times 71 = \textbf{213}$ marbles

10. The model that involves ratio

Aaron buys a tie and a belt. The prices of the tie and belt are in the ratio 2 : 5. If both items cost $539,

(a) what is the price of the tie?

(b) what is the price of the belt?

$\$539 \div 7 = \$77$

Tie (2 units) → $2 \times \$77 = \textbf{\$154}$

Belt (5 units) → $5 \times \$77 = \textbf{\$385}$

11. The model that involves comparison of fractions

Jack's height is $\frac{2}{3}$ of Leslie's height. Leslie's height is $\frac{3}{4}$ of Lindsay's height. If Lindsay is 160 cm tall, find Jack's height and Leslie's height.

1 unit → $160 \div 4 = 40$ cm

Leslie's height (3 units) → $3 \times 40 = \textbf{120 cm}$

Jack's height (2 units) → $2 \times 40 = \textbf{80 cm}$

Thinking skills and strategies are important in mathematical problem solving. These skills are applied when students think through the math problems to solve them. Below are some commonly used thinking skills and strategies applied in mathematical problem solving.

1. Comparing

Comparing is a form of thinking skill that students can apply to identify similarities and differences.

When comparing numbers, look carefully at each digit before deciding if a number is greater or less than the other. Students might also use a number line for comparison when there are more numbers.

Example:

3 is greater than 2 but smaller than 7.

2. Sequencing

A sequence shows the order of a series of numbers. *Sequencing* is a form of thinking skill that requires students to place numbers in a particular order. There are many terms in a sequence. The terms refer to the numbers in a sequence.

To place numbers in a correct order, students must first find a rule that generates the sequence. In a simple math sequence, students can either add or subtract to find the unknown terms in the sequence.

Example: Find the 7th term in the sequence below.

1,	4,	7,	10,	13,	16	?
1st term	2nd term	3rd term	4th term	5th term	6th term	7th term

Step 1: This sequence is in an increasing order.

Step 2: $4 - 1 = 3$ $7 - 4 = 3$
The difference between two consecutive terms is 3.

Step 3: $16 + 3 = 19$
The 7th term is **19**.

3. Visualization

Visualization is a problem solving strategy that can help students visualize a problem through the use of physical objects. Students will play a more active role in solving the problem by manipulating these objects.

The main advantage of using this strategy is the mobility of information in the process of solving the problem. When students make a wrong step in the process, they can retrace the step without erasing or canceling it.

The other advantage is that this strategy helps develop a better understanding of the problem or solution through visual objects or images. In this way, students will be better able to remember how to solve these types of problems.

Singapore Math Practice Level 4A

Some of the commonly used objects for this strategy are toothpicks, straws, cards, strings, water, sand, pencils, paper, and dice.

4. Look for a Pattern

This strategy requires the use of observational and analytical skills. Students have to observe the given data to find a pattern in order to solve the problem. Math word problems that involve the use of this strategy usually have repeated numbers or patterns.

Example: Find the sum of all the numbers from 1 to 100.

Step 1: Simplify the problem.

Find the sum of 1, 2, 3, 4, 5, 6, 7, 8, 9, and 10.

Step 2: Look for a pattern.

1 + 10 = 11	2 + 9 = 11	3 + 8 = 11
4 + 7 = 11	5 + 6 = 11	

Step 3: Describe the pattern.

When finding the sum of 1 to 10, add the first and last numbers to get a result of 11. Then, add the second and second last numbers to get the same result. The pattern continues until all the numbers from 1 to 10 are added. There will be 5 pairs of such results. Since each addition equals 11, the answer is then $5 \times 11 = 55$.

Step 4: Use the pattern to find the answer.

Since there are 5 pairs in the sum of 1 to 10, there should be ($10 \times 5 = 50$ pairs) in the sum of 1 to 100.

Note that the addition for each pair is not equal to 11 now. The addition for each pair is now ($1 + 100 = 101$).

$$50 \times 101 = 5050$$

The sum of all the numbers from 1 to 100 is **5,050**.

5. Working Backward

The strategy of working backward applies only to a specific type of math word problem. These word problems state the end result, and students are required to find the total number. In order to solve these word problems, students have to work backward by thinking through the correct sequence of events. The strategy of working backward allows students to use their logical reasoning and sequencing to find the answers.

Example: Sarah has a piece of ribbon. She cuts the ribbon into 4 equal parts. Each part is then cut into 3 smaller equal parts. If the length of each small part is 35 cm, how long is the piece of ribbon?

$$3 \times 35 = 105 \text{ cm}$$
$$4 \times 105 = 420 \text{ cm}$$

The piece of ribbon is **420 cm**.

6. The Before-After Concept

The *Before-After* concept lists all the relevant data before and after an event. Students can then compare the differences and eventually solve the problems. Usually, the Before-After concept and the mathematical model go hand in hand to solve math word problems. Note that the Before-After concept can be applied only to a certain type of math word problem, which trains students to think sequentially.

Example: Kelly has 4 times as much money as Joey. After Kelly uses some money to buy a tennis racquet, and Joey uses $30 to buy a pair of pants, Kelly has twice as much money as Joey. If Joey has $98 in the beginning,
(a) how much money does Kelly have in the end?
(b) how much money does Kelly spend on the tennis racquet?

Before

After

(a) $98 - $30 = $68
$2 \times $68 = 136
Kelly has **$136** in the end.

(b) $4 \times $98 = 392
$392 - $136 = 256
Kelly spends **$256** on the tennis racquet.

7. Making Supposition

Making supposition is commonly known as "making an assumption." Students can use this strategy to solve certain types of math word problems. Making assumptions will eliminate some possibilities and simplifies the word problems by providing a boundary of values to work within.

Example: Mrs. Jackson bought 100 pieces of candy for all the students in her class. How many pieces of candy would each student receive if there were 25 students in her class?

In the above word problem, assume that each student received the same number of pieces. This eliminates the possibilities that some students would receive more than others due to good behaviour, better results, or any other reason.

8. Representation of Problem

In problem solving, students often use representations in the solutions to show their understanding of the problems. Using representations also allow students to understand the mathematical concepts and relationships as well as to manipulate the information presented in the problems. Examples of representations are diagrams and lists or tables.

Diagrams allow students to consolidate or organize the information given in the problems. By drawing a diagram, students can see the problem clearly and solve it effectively.

A list or table can help students organize information that is useful for analysis. After analyzing, students can then see a pattern, which can be used to solve the problem.

9. Guess and Check

One of the most important and effective problem-solving techniques is *Guess and Check*. It is also known as *Trial and Error*. As the name suggests, students have to guess the answer to a problem and check if that guess is correct. If the guess is wrong, students will make another guess. This will continue until the guess is correct.

It is beneficial to keep a record of all the guesses and checks in a table. In addition, a *Comments* column can be included. This will enable students to analyze their guess (if it is too high or too low) and improve on the next guess. Be careful; this problem-solving technique can be tiresome without systematic or logical guesses.

Example: Jessica had 15 coins. Some of them were 10-cent coins and the rest were 5-cent coins. The total amount added up to $1.25. How many coins of each kind were there?

Use the guess-and-check method.

Number of 10¢ Coins	Value	Number of 5¢ Coins	Value	Total Number of Coins	Total Value
7	7 × 10¢ = 70¢	8	8 × 5¢ = 40¢	7 + 8 = 15	70¢ + 40¢ = 110¢ = $1.10
8	8 × 10¢ = 80¢	7	7 × 5¢ = 35¢	8 + 7 = 15	80¢ + 35¢ = 115¢ = $1.15
10	10 × 10¢ = 100¢	5	5 × 5¢ = 25¢	10 + 5 = 15	100¢ + 25¢ = 125¢ = $1.25

There were **ten** 10-cent coins and **five** 5-cent coins.

10. Restate the Problem

When solving challenging math problems, conventional methods may not be workable. Instead, restating the problem will enable students to see some challenging problems in a different light so that they can better understand them.

The strategy of restating the problem is to "say" the problem in a different and clearer way. However, students have to ensure that the main idea of the problem is not altered.

How do students restate a math problem?

First, read and understand the problem. Gather the given facts and unknowns. Note any condition(s) that have to be satisfied.

Next, restate the problem. Imagine narrating this problem to a friend. Present the given facts, unknown(s), and condition(s). Students may want to write the "revised" problem. Once the "revised" problem is analyzed, students should be able to think of an appropriate strategy to solve it.

11. Simplify the Problem

One of the commonly used strategies in mathematical problem solving is simplification of the problem. When a problem is simplified, it can be "broken down" into two or more smaller parts. Students can then solve the parts systematically to get to the final answer.

Singapore Math Practice Level 4A

Table of Contents

Singapore Math Practice Level 4A

LEARNING OUTCOMES

Unit 1   Whole Numbers (Part 1)
Students should be able to
- recognize and write numbers up to 100,000 in numerals and words.
- identify the correct place value.
- compare and arrange numbers up to 100,000.
- complete number patterns.

Unit 2   Whole Numbers (Part 2)
Students should be able to
- round numbers to the nearest ten or hundred.
- estimate answers involving 4 operations.
- list factors or multiples of a whole number.
- find common factors or multiples.

Review 1
This review tests students' understanding of Units 1 & 2.

Unit 3   Whole Numbers (Part 3)
Students should be able to
- multiply numbers by 1-digit and 2-digit numbers.
- divide numbers by 1-digit numbers.
- estimate answers in multiplication and division.
- check that answers are reasonable.
- solve up to 3-step story problems.

Unit 4   Line Graphs and Tables
Students should be able to
- read and understand tables and line graphs.
- complete tables using given data.
- solve problems using given data in tables and line graphs.

Review 2
This review tests students' understanding of Units 3 & 4.

Unit 5   Fractions
Students should be able to
- recognize mixed numbers and improper fractions.
- convert mixed numbers to improper fractions or improper fractions to mixed numbers.
- add and subtract fractions.
- multiply proper/improper fractions and whole numbers.
- solve up to 2-step story problems related to fractions.

Unit 6   Angles
Students should be able to
- name angles.
- measure and draw angles in degrees with the use of a protractor.
- relate a turn with degrees up to 360°.
- understand 8-point compass.

Review 3
This review tests students' understanding of Units 5 & 6.

Unit 7   Perpendicular and Parallel Lines
Students should be able to
- draw and identify perpendicular and parallel lines.
- identify vertical and horizontal lines.

Unit 8   Rectangles and Squares
Students should be able to
- recognize properties of rectangles and squares.
- find unknown lengths in rectangles and squares.
- find unknown angles in rectangles and squares.

Review 4
This review tests students' understanding of Units 7 & 8.

Final Review
This review is an excellent assessment of students' understanding of all the topics in this book.

Singapore Math Practice Level 4A

FORMULA SHEET

Unit 1 Whole Numbers (Part 1)

5-digit numbers can be written in this manner.

Example: Write 72,948 as words.
seventy-two thousand, nine hundred, forty-eight

Place value

In a 5-digit number, each digit is in a different place and has a different value. The place value will help identify the particular place such as ten thousands, thousands, hundreds, tens, or ones and its value.

Example: In 16,258,
the digit 1 is in the **ten thousands** place.
the digit 1 stands for **10 thousands** or **10,000**.
the value of the digit 1 is **10,000**.

Comparing numbers

Start comparing the 2 numbers from the ten thousands place.

- When one number is bigger than the other, use the words *greater than* to describe it.
- When one number is smaller than the other, use the words *smaller than* to describe it.

More than and Less than

Substitute the words *more than* with an addition sign (**+**).

Example: What is 20,000 more than 58,324?
20,000 + 58,324 = 78,324

Similarly, substitute the words *less than* with a subtraction sign (**–**).

Example: What is 9,000 less than 12,685?
12,685 – 9,000 = 3,685

Order and Pattern

When arranging a set of numbers in order,

- determine if the order must begin with the largest or the smallest,
- compare the place value of the numbers,
- arrange the numbers in the correct order.

For number pattern problems,

- determine if the number pattern is in an increasing or a decreasing order,
- find the difference between 2 consecutive numbers,
- apply the difference to find the unknown number.

Unit 2 Whole Numbers (Part 2)

Rounding is to express a number to its nearest ten, hundred, or thousand.
Symbol: approximation sign ($\approx$)
Step 1: Identify the digit to observe.
Step 2: If the digit is less than 5, round down to a lower number.
Step 3: If the digit is equal to or more than 5, round up to a higher number.
Examples: $936 \approx 940$ (when rounded off to the nearest ten)
≈ 900 (when rounded off to the nearest hundred)

Estimation gives an approximate calculation when performing addition, subtraction, multiplication, or division.

Estimation in addition/subtraction

Step 1: Round the addends/minuends/subtrahends to the nearest ten or hundred.
Step 2: Add the rounded addends/minuends/subtrahends.
Examples: $56 + 93 \approx 60 + 90 = 150$
$81 – 25 \approx 80 – 30 = 50$

Estimation in multiplication

Step 1: Round the multiplicand to the nearest ten or hundred.
Step 2: Multiply the rounded multiplicand by the multiplier.
Example: $68 \times 5 \approx 70 \times 5 = 350$

Estimation in division

Step 1: Round the dividend to the nearest number for easy division.
Step 2: Divide the rounded dividend by the divisor to get the final answer.
Example: $731 \div 9 \approx 720 \div 9 = 80$

A **factor** is a number that can be divided into another number exactly.
dividend ÷ factor = quotient

A factor can also be a multiplicand or multiplier.
factor × factor = product
Example: The factors of 14 are 1, 2, 7, and 14.

A **multiple** is obtained by multiplying a number by another number.
factor × factor = multiple
Example: The multiples of 5 are 5, 10, 15, 20, 25, 30, …

Unit 3 Whole Numbers (Part 3)

Multiply 4-digit number by 1-digit number

- Multiply the digit in the ones place by the multiplier. Regroup the ones if required.
- Multiply the digit in the tens place by the multiplier. Regroup the tens if required.
- Multiply the digit in the hundreds place by the multiplier. Regroup the hundreds if required.
- Multiply the digit in the thousands place by the multiplier. Regroup the thousands if required.

Multiply 3-digit number by 2-digit number

Method 1

If the multiplier is in tens, break down the multiplier into smaller parts for easy multiplication.

Example:
$420 \times 40 = 420 \times 4 \times 10 = 1,680 \times 10 = 16,800$

Method 2

Step 1: Multiply the digit in the ones place by the digit in the ones place of the multiplier. Regroup the ones if required.
Multiply the digit in the tens place by the digit in the ones place of the multiplier. Regroup the tens if required.
Multiply the digit in the hundreds place by the digit in the ones place of the multiplier. Regroup the hundreds if required.
Step 2: Multiply the digit in the ones place by the tens of the multiplier. Regroup the ones if required.

Multiply the digit in the tens place by the tens of the multiplier. Regroup the tens if required.

Multiply the digit in the hundreds place by the tens of the multiplier. Regroup the hundreds if required.

Step 3: Add the results obtained in Steps 1 and 2 to get the final answer.

<u>Divide 4-digit number by 1-digit number</u>

Step 1: Divide the digit in the thousands place by the divisor. If there is a remainder, regroup the hundreds.

Step 2: Divide the hundreds by the divisor. If there is a remainder, regroup the tens.

Step 3: Divide the tens by the divisor. If there is a remainder, regroup the ones.

Step 4: Divide the ones by the divisor. Find the remainder if there is any.

Unit 4 Line Graphs and Tables

<u>Tables</u>

A table can consolidate data in a clear and organized manner. Use the data collected from a bar graph to complete a table. Also use the data given in the table to solve problems.

Examples:

Types of dessert	Number of customers
Apple Pie	22
Brownie	30
Chocolate Cake	10
Key Lime Pie	8

Types of dessert	Apple Pie	Brownie	Chocolate Cake	Key Lime Pie
Number of customers	22	30	10	8

<u>Line Graphs</u>

A line graph is another way to present data in an organized manner. Use the information given in line graphs to solve problems.

Example:

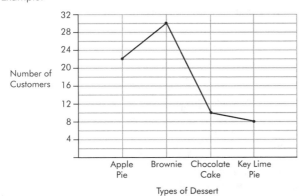

Unit 5 Fractions

A **mixed number** consists of a whole number and a fraction.

Examples: $1\frac{1}{2}$, $2\frac{1}{4}$, $5\frac{2}{5}$

An **improper fraction** is a fraction where its numerator is greater than its denominator.

Examples: $\frac{6}{5}$, $\frac{9}{7}$, $\frac{16}{7}$

<u>Reducing fractions to their simplest form</u>

Use the method of cancellation to reduce a fraction to its lowest term. Just divide both numerator and denominator by the same number. Ensure that such division does not have any remainder.

Example: $3\frac{4 \div 2}{6 \div 2} = 3\frac{2}{3}$

<u>Convert a mixed number to an improper fraction</u>

- Break the mixed number down into a whole number and a fraction.
- Convert the whole number to an improper fraction. Ensure both fractions have the same denominator.
- Add the numerator of both fractions.
- Reduce to its simplest form if needed.

Example: $6\frac{3}{8} = 6 + \frac{3}{8} = \frac{48}{8} + \frac{3}{8} = \frac{51}{8}$

<u>Convert an improper fraction to a mixed number</u>

Method 1

- Break the improper fraction down into the whole number in fractional form and the fraction.
- Convert the whole number in fractional form to a whole number.
- Reduce the other fraction to its simplest form if needed.
- Add the whole number and fraction.

Example: $\frac{27}{7} = \frac{21}{7} + \frac{6}{7} = 3 + \frac{6}{7} = 3\frac{6}{7}$

Method 2

- Divide the numerator by denominator.
- The quotient will be the whole number.
- The remainder will be numerator of the fraction.
- The divisor will be denominator of the fraction.

Example: $\frac{27}{7} = 27 \div 7 = 3\frac{6}{7}$

$$7\overline{)27} \\ \underline{21} \\ 6$$

<u>Adding fractions</u>

- Make sure the denominators of all fractions are common.
- Add all numerators.
- Reduce the final fraction to its simplest form.
- Convert an improper fraction to a mixed number if needed.

Example: $\frac{6}{9} + \frac{1}{3} = \frac{6}{9} + \frac{3}{9} = \frac{9}{9} = 1$

<u>Subtracting fractions</u>

- Make sure the denominators of all fractions are common.
- Subtract all numerators.
- Reduce the final fraction to its simplest form.
- Convert an improper fraction to a mixed number if needed.

Example: $4 - \frac{4}{7} = 3\frac{7}{7} - \frac{4}{7} = 3\frac{3}{7}$

<u>Finding the fraction of a set</u>

- Multiply the numerator by the whole number.
- The denominator remains the same.
- Reduce the fraction to its simplest form if needed.

Example: $\frac{4}{5}$ of $20 = \frac{4}{5} \times 20 = \frac{80}{5} = 16$

Unit 6 Angles

Vertex is a point whereby two lines meet to form an angle. The lines and vertex are labelled using a capital letter.

Singapore Math Practice Level 4A

Example:

The name of the angle is ∠XYZ or ∠ZYX.

Alternatively, a small letter can represent an angle. In this example, it will be ∠a.

Measuring an angle

Use a protractor to measure an angle.

Symbol: degrees (°)

Step 1: Place the base line of a protractor on one of the lines of the angle.

Step 2: Place the center of the protractor at the vertex.

Step 3: Always read from 0°. The reading is obtained when the second line of the angle meets the marking on the protractor.

Drawing an angle

Step 1: Draw a horizontal line and mark a point centrally.

Step 2: Place the base line of a protractor on the line and the center of the protractor on the marked point.

Step 3: Measure from 0°. Mark a dot at the correct measurement. Draw a straight line through the dot to meet the horizontal line. An angle is formed.

Turns and right angles

1 right angle	$\frac{1}{4}$ of a complete turn	90°
2 right angles	$\frac{1}{2}$ of a complete turn	180°
3 right angles	$\frac{3}{4}$ of a complete turn	270°
4 right angles	1 complete turn	360°

Clockwise moves in the same direction as the movement of the clock.

Counterclockwise moves in the opposite direction as the movement of the clock.

8-point compass

Unit 7 Perpendicular and Parallel Lines

Drawing a pair of perpendicular lines

Step 1: Use a ruler to draw a straight line. Label this line as XY.

Step 2: Place a set-square on the line and draw a vertical line. Label this line as AB.

Drawing a pair of parallel lines

Step 1: Use a ruler to draw a straight line. Label this line as AB.

Step 2: Place a set-square on the line. Next, place a ruler next to the set-square.

Step 3: Move the set-square along the ruler. Draw a line along the set-square. Label this line as CD.

Horizontal line is a straight line that runs left and right, like the x-axis.

Example: _____

Vertical line is a line that runs up and down, like the y-axis.

Example:

Unit 8 Rectangles and Squares

Properties of a square

1. A square has four sides.
2. All four sides are equal.
3. It has two pairs of parallel lines.
4. All four angles are right angles.

Properties of a rectangle

1. A rectangle has four sides.
2. Its opposite sides are equal.
3. It has two pairs of parallel lines.
4. All four angles are right angles.

Singapore Math Practice Level 4A

Unit 1: WHOLE NUMBERS (PART 1)

Examples:

1. What does the digit 4 stand for in 71,439?

    <u>4 hundreds</u> or <u>**400**</u>

2. What is 50,000 more than 8,395?

    $50,000 + 8,395 = \underline{\textbf{58,395}}$

3. Complete the number pattern.

    78,436, <u>**79,486**</u>, 80,536, 81,586

    $81,586 - 80,536 = 1,050$

    $78,436 + 1,050 = 79,486$

Write the following numbers as words on the lines.

1. 23,701 _____

2. 40,825 _____

3. 68,090 _____

4. 55,002 _____

5. 14,011 _____

Write the correct numbers in numerals on the lines.

6. eleven thousand, six hundred, two   _____

7. ninety-two thousand, three hundred, fourteen   _____

8. fifty-seven thousand, twelve   _____

9. sixty thousand, two hundred, forty-five   _____

10. eighty-two thousand, one   _____

Write the correct value of each digit in its box.

11. 15,326

13. 78,035

12. 58,217

14. 81,420

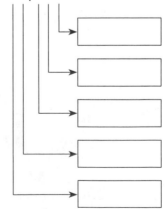

Fill in each blank with the correct answer.

15. In 64,925, the digit 6 is in the _____ place.

16. In 80,647, the digit 4 is in the _____ place.

17. In 38,416, the digit _____ is in the thousands place.

18. In 73,029, the digit _____ is in the hundreds place.

19. In 81,246,

    (a)   the digit 8 stands for _____.

    (b)   the digit 1 stands for _____.

    (c)   the digit 2 stands for _____.

    (d)   the digit 4 stands for _____.

    (e)   the digit 6 stands for _____.

20. 5,217 = 5 thousands + _____ hundreds + 1 ten + 7 ones

21. 1,106 = 1 thousand + _____ hundred + 6 ones

22. 35,248 = _____ ten thousands + 5 thousands + 2 hundreds + 4 tens + 8 ones

23. 50,364 = 5 ten thousands + 3 hundreds + _____ tens + 4 ones

24. 63,724 = 60,000 + _____ + 700 + 20 + 4

25. 30,517 = 30,000 + 500 + _____ + 7

26. 10,000 + _____ + 100 = 19,100

27. 3,000 + _____ + 30 + 6 = 3,136

28. 88,627 = _____ + 8,000 + 600 + 20 + 7

Singapore Math Practice Level 4A

29. Circle the greater number.

                48,165   49,561

30. Circle the greater number.

                98,075   97,085

31. Circle the smaller number.

                13,986   13,689

32. Circle the smaller number.

                10,738   9,173

Arrange the following numbers in ascending order.

33. 5,931,   1,359,   1,593,   5,319

_____

34. 14,632,   41,562,   24,163,   12,643

_____

35. 6,845,   4,586,   8,564,   4,685

_____

Arrange the following numbers in descending order.

36. 7,014,   1,407,   7,410,   1,740

_____

37. 39,628,   26,983,   63,892,   96,268

_____

38. 2,653,   3,652,   5,236,   5,362

_____

Complete the number patterns.

39. 226, 246, 266, _____, _____

40. 33,045, 33,050, _____, _____, 33,065

41. _____, 7,540, 7,550, _____, 7,570

42. 87,455, 88,455, 89,455, _____, _____

Fill in each blank with the correct answer.

43. _____ is 100 less than 43,112.

44. _____ is 20 less than 94,606.

45. _____ is 2,000 more than 18,096.

46. _____ is 1,000 more than 80,493.

47. 3,000 less than 21,475 is _____.

48. 100 less than 10,000 is _____.

49. 6,000 more than 4,381 is _____.

50. 99 more than 90,000 is _____.

Singapore Math Practice Level 4A

Unit 2: WHOLE NUMBERS (PART 2)

Examples:

1. Round 798 to the nearest hundred.

    $798 \approx \underline{\textbf{800}}$

2. Estimate the value of $351 - 87$.

    $351 - 87 \approx 350 - 90 = \underline{\textbf{260}}$

3. Estimate the value of $384 \div 8$.

    $384 \div 8 \approx 400 \div 8 = \underline{\textbf{50}}$

4. Find all the factors of 40.

    $40 = 1 \times 40$
    $40 = 2 \times 20$
    $40 = 4 \times 10$
    $40 = 5 \times 8$

    The factors of 40 are $\underline{1}$, $\underline{2}$, $\underline{4}$, $\underline{5}$, $\underline{8}$, $\underline{10}$, $\underline{20}$, and $\underline{40}$.

5. Find the first five multiples of 8.

    $\underline{8}$, $\underline{16}$, $\underline{24}$, $\underline{32}$, and $\underline{40}$

Singapore Math Practice Level 4A

Round the following numbers to the nearest ten.

1. 771   ≈ _____

2. 848   ≈ _____

3. 661   ≈ _____

4. 296   ≈ _____

5. 1,087 ≈ _____

6. 1,782 ≈ _____

7. 39,917 ≈ _____

8. 46,547 ≈ _____

9. 11,201 ≈ _____

10. 59,999 ≈ _____

Round the following numbers to the nearest hundred.

11. 536   ≈ _____

12. 881   ≈ _____

13. 3,084 ≈ _____

14. 1,117 ≈ _____

15. 6,944 ≈ _____

16. 89,544 ≈ _____

17. 23,891 ≈ _____

18. 12,057 ≈ _____

19. 61,272 ≈ _____

20. 74,808 ≈ _____

Round the following numbers to the nearest ten and estimate their values.

21. 36 + 12 ≈ _____

22. 672 + 48 ≈ _____

23. 66 + 725 ≈ _____

24. 932 – 19 ≈ _____

25. 419 – 38 ≈ _____

26. 519 – 21 ≈ _____

Singapore Math Practice Level 4A

Estimate the value.

27. 48×8 ≈ _____

28. 25×7 ≈ _____

29. $301 - 9$ ≈ _____

30. $697 - 88$ ≈ _____

31. $118 \div 4$ ≈ _____

32. $324 \div 5$ ≈ _____

33. $463 + 93 + 551$ ≈ _____

34. $876 + 121 + 43$ ≈ _____

Fill in each blank with the correct answer.

35. 12 = _____ × _____

    12 = _____ × _____

    12 = _____ × _____

The factors of 12 are _____, _____, _____, _____, _____, and _____.

36. 42 = _____ × _____

    42 = _____ × _____

    42 = _____ × _____

    42 = _____ × _____

The factors of 42 are _____, _____, _____, _____, _____, _____, _____, and _____.

Singapore Math Practice Level 4A

37. $36 = \underline{\hspace{3em}} \times \underline{\hspace{3em}}$

    $36 = \underline{\hspace{3em}} \times \underline{\hspace{3em}}$

    $36 = \underline{\hspace{3em}} \times \underline{\hspace{3em}}$

    $36 = \underline{\hspace{3em}} \times \underline{\hspace{3em}}$

    $36 = \underline{\hspace{3em}} \times \underline{\hspace{3em}}$

    The factors of 36 are ____, ____, ____, ____, ____, ____, ____, ____, and ____.

38. (a) The factors of 8 are _____.

    (b) The factors of 16 are _____.

    (c) The common factors of 8 and 16 are _____.

39. (a) The factors of 14 are _____.

    (b) The factors of 28 are _____.

    (c) The common factors of 14 and 28 are _____.

40. (a) The factors of 9 are _____.

    (b) The factors of 18 are _____.

    (c) The common factors of 9 and 18 are _____.

41. The first four multiples of 5 are ____, ____, ____, and ____.

42. The first three multiples of 9 are ____, ____, and ____.

43. The third multiple of 6 is ____.

44. The seventh multiple of 5 is ____.

45. (a) The first six multiples of 2 are ____, ____, ____, ____, ____, and ____.

Singapore Math Practice Level 4A

(b) The first six multiples of 3 are _____, _____, _____, _____, _____, and _____.

(c) The two common multiples of 2 and 3 are _____ and _____.

46. (a) The first six multiples of 4 are _____, _____, _____, _____, _____, and _____.

(b) The first six multiples of 8 are _____, _____, _____, _____, _____, and _____.

(c) The three common multiples of 4 and 8 are _____, _____, and _____.

Write your answers on the lines.

47. A train traveled 13,769 km from City A to City B. Then, it traveled another 25,325 km to City C. What was the estimated distance traveled by the train from City A to City C? Round each number to the nearest hundred and estimate the value.

_____

48. A number, when added to 7,982, is 25,000. Round this number to the nearest ten.

_____

49. There were 1,345 books left in a bookstore. If the shopkeeper had sold 7,609 books in the past month, how many books were in the bookstore at first? Round the answer to the nearest ten.

_____

50. In a school, there are 1,124 students in the morning session. There are 259 more students in the afternoon session than in the morning session. How many students are in the school when rounded to the nearest hundred?

_____

Singapore Math Practice Level 4A

51. What is the smallest two-digit number that has only 4 factors?

_____

52. 8 is a factor of number X. It is between 50 and 60. What is number X?

_____

53. Number Y is a multiple of 8. It is between 20 and 30. It is also a factor of 48. What is number Y?

_____

54. If 32 is the fourth multiple of a number, what is the number?

_____

55. The two common multiples of 2 one-digit numbers are 14 and 28. If 1 is not the answer, what are the 2 one-digit numbers?

_____

REVIEW 1

Choose the correct answer. Write its number in the parentheses.

1. Which of the following shows the correct numeral for seventy-two thousand, eight hundred, forty-five?

    (1) 72,845   (3) 78,245

    (2) 72,854   (4) 78,254   (   )

2. The digit 8 in 28,095 stands for _____.

    (1) 8 ten thousands   (3) 8 hundreds

    (2) 8 thousands   (4) 8 tens   (   )

3. Which of the following is **not** a common multiple of 8 and 6?

    (1) 18   (3) 72

    (2) 24   (4) 144   (   )

4. Round each number to the nearest ten and estimate the value of 1,987 + 5,248.

    (1) 7,220   (3) 7,240

    (2) 7,230   (4) 7,250   (   )

5. Which of the following is a common factor of 28 and 36?

    (1) 3   (3) 6

    (2) 4   (4) 8   (   )

6. 9,050, _____, 7,030, 6,020, 5,010.

    What is the missing number in the pattern?

    (1) 8,020   (3) 8,040

    (2) 8,030   (4) 8,050   (   )

24

7. Which of the following has the greatest value?

   (1) 2,000 less than 10,000 (3) 2,000 more than 1,000
   (2) 2,000 less than 8,000   (4) 2,000 more than 800   (   )

8. Which of the following shows the first four multiples of 7?

   (1) 7, 14, 20, 27   (3) 7, 14, 28, 35
   (2) 7, 14, 21, 28   (4) 7, 14, 28, 42   (   )

9. 49,753 = _____ + 9 thousands + 7 hundreds + 5 tens + 3 ones

   (1) 400 ten thousands   (3) 4 ten thousands
   (2) 40 ten thousands   (4) 4 thousands   (   )

10. Estimate the value of 404 × 9.

   (1) 3,600   (3) 3,645
   (2) 3,636   (4) 4,000   (   )

Write your answers on the lines.

11. Write 49,005 in words.

   _____

12. In 94,857, the digit 4 is in the ☐ place.   _____

13. Arrange these numbers in ascending order.

   15,050,   15,005,   15,500

   _____

14. Round each number to the nearest ten and estimate its value.

   559 + 19 + 942 ≈ ☐   _____

Singapore Math Practice Level 4A

15. The seventh multiple of 9 is ☐.

     _____

16. Round 89,091 to the nearest hundred.

     _____

17. 50 thousands + 90 tens + 7 ones = ☐

     _____

18. List all the factors of 45.

     _____

19. Add 18,360 and 2,598. The digit ☐ is in the thousands place.

     _____

20. List the first two common multiples of 4 and 6.

     _____

Unit 3: WHOLE NUMBERS (PART 3)

Examples:

1.
$$
\begin{array}{r}
\overset{4\ \ 5}{8{,}0\,4\,6} \\
\times 9 \\
\hline
7\,2{,}4\,1\,4 \\
\end{array}
$$

2.
$$
\begin{array}{r}
\overset{\overset{1\ \ 1}{5\ \ 6}}{3\,6\,8} \\
\times 2\,8 \\
\hline
2\,9\,4\,4 \\
7\,3\,6 \\
\hline
1\,0{,}3\,0\,4 \\
\end{array}
$$

3.
$$
\begin{array}{r}
1{,}5\,5\,7 \\
6\,)\overline{9{,}3\,4\,2} \\
\underline{6} \\
3\,3 \\
\underline{3\,0} \\
3\,4 \\
\underline{3\,0} \\
4\,2 \\
\underline{4\,2} \\
0 \\
\end{array}
$$

27

Singapore Math Practice Level 4A

Solve the following problems. Show your work.

1.
$$\begin{array}{r} 412 \\ \times \quad 4 \\ \hline \end{array}$$

6.
$$\begin{array}{r} 5,317 \\ \times \quad 6 \\ \hline \end{array}$$

2.
$$\begin{array}{r} 547 \\ \times \quad 2 \\ \hline \end{array}$$

7.
$$\begin{array}{r} 2,011 \\ \times \quad 8 \\ \hline \end{array}$$

3.
$$\begin{array}{r} 610 \\ \times \quad 5 \\ \hline \end{array}$$

8.
$$\begin{array}{r} 6,028 \\ \times \quad 9 \\ \hline \end{array}$$

4.
$$\begin{array}{r} 935 \\ \times \quad 3 \\ \hline \end{array}$$

9.
$$\begin{array}{r} 1,526 \\ \times \quad 5 \\ \hline \end{array}$$

5.
$$\begin{array}{r} 109 \\ \times \quad 7 \\ \hline \end{array}$$

10.
$$\begin{array}{r} 8,437 \\ \times \quad 8 \\ \hline \end{array}$$

Singapore Math Practice Level 4A

11. $\begin{array}{r} 46 \\ \times\ 18 \\ \hline \end{array}$

12. $\begin{array}{r} 35 \\ \times\ 20 \\ \hline \end{array}$

13. $\begin{array}{r} 67 \\ \times\ 36 \\ \hline \end{array}$

14. $\begin{array}{r} 91 \\ \times\ 27 \\ \hline \end{array}$

15. $\begin{array}{r} 89 \\ \times\ 16 \\ \hline \end{array}$

16. $\begin{array}{r} 126 \\ \times\ 50 \\ \hline \end{array}$

17. $\begin{array}{r} 625 \\ \times\ 73 \\ \hline \end{array}$

18. $\begin{array}{r} 619 \\ \times\ 24 \\ \hline \end{array}$

19. $\begin{array}{r} 281 \\ \times\ 53 \\ \hline \end{array}$

20. $\begin{array}{r} 380 \\ \times\ 36 \\ \hline \end{array}$

Singapore Math Practice Level 4A

Solve the following problems. Show your work.

21. $5\overline{)1,355}$

24. $8\overline{)6,088}$

22. $3\overline{)4,827}$

25. $6\overline{)1,458}$

23. $2\overline{)9,804}$

26. $3\overline{)1,131}$

Fill in each blank with the correct answer.

27. $18 \times 20 = $ _____ $\times$ _____ tens

$= $ _____ tens

$= $ _____

28. $69 \times 40 = $ _____ $\times$ _____ tens

$= $ _____ tens

$= $ _____

30

29. $98 \times 30 = $ _____ $\times$ _____ tens

= _____ tens

= _____

30. $53 \times 60 = $ _____ $\times$ _____ $\times 10$

= _____ $\times 10$

= _____

31. $77 \times 90 = $ _____ $\times$ _____ $\times 10$

= _____ $\times 10$

= _____

32. $42 \times 80 = $ _____ $\times$ _____ $\times 10$

= _____ $\times 10$

= _____

33. $4,569 \div 8 = $ _____ R _____

34. $1,348 \div 5 = $ _____ R _____

35. $4,240 \div 7 = $ _____ R _____

36. $3,134 \div 4 = $ _____ R _____

37. $9,381 \div 9 = $ _____ R _____

38. $59 \times 17 \approx $ _____ $\times$ _____

= _____

31

Singapore Math Practice Level 4A

39. $623 \times 55 \approx$ _____ $\times$ _____

           $=$ _____

40. $917 \times 31 \approx$ _____ $\times$ _____

           $=$ _____

41. $237 \div 5 \approx$ _____ $\div 5$

           $=$ _____

42. $4,927 \div 7 \approx$ _____ $\div 7$

           $=$ _____

43. $8,080 \div 9 \approx$ _____ $\div 9$

           $=$ _____

44. (a) Multiply 84 by 52. _____

    (b) Estimate the value of 84×52. _____

    (c) State if your actual answer is reasonable. _____

45. (a) Multiply 409 by 93. _____

    (b) Estimate the value of 409×93. _____

    (c) State if your actual answer is reasonable. _____

46. (a) Multiply 976 by 38. _____

    (b) Estimate the value of 976×38. _____

    (c) State if your actual answer is reasonable. _____

47. (a) Divide 43 by 8. _____

(b) Estimate the value of 43 ÷ 8. _____

(c) State if your actual answer is reasonable. _____

48. (a) Divide 538 by 6. _____

(b) Estimate the value of 538 ÷ 6. _____

(c) State if your actual answer is reasonable. _____

49. (a) Divide 8,765 by 4. _____

(b) Estimate the value of 8,765 ÷ 4. _____

(c) State if your actual answer is reasonable. _____

Solve the following story problems. Show your work in the space below.

50. There are 255 balloons in a package. How many balloons are there in a dozen packages?

Singapore Math Practice Level 4A

51. A factory makes 2,275 watches in a week. How many watches does it make in 3 days?

52. A shirt costs $253 and a tie costs $78. David bought 4 shirts and 3 ties. How much did he spend altogether?

53. A purse costs 4 times as much as a dress. If the purse costs $276, how much does Anna spend on the purse and 3 dresses?

54. Jason had some marbles. He gave 35 marbles to each of his 4 brothers and still had 219 marbles left. How many marbles did Jason have to begin with?

55. 114 men and 686 women went to a concert. Each ticket cost $17. How much money was collected in all?

56. A baker bakes 840 loaves of bread in a day. How many loaves of bread will he bake in 6 weeks?

Singapore Math Practice Level 4A

57. Cecilia has 896 stickers. She gives 50 stickers to seven of her friends. She sorts the remaining stickers equally into three albums. How many stickers are there in each album?

58. There were 400 pieces of candy in a package. The principal of a school bought 25 packages for 2,000 children on Halloween.

    (a) How many pieces of candy did the principal buy altogether?

    (b) If each child was given 7 pieces, how many more packages were needed?

59. Kimi is 16 years old and her mother is 44 years old this year. How many years ago was Kimi's mother five times as old as Kimi?

60. A stereo costs $328. A television set costs four times as much as the stereo. Mr. Simon buys the stereo and the television set and pays for them in eight monthly installments. How much must he pay for them each month?

61. Michael had $3,600. After spending $320, he still had twice as much as Cynthia. Find the total amount of money they had in the beginning.

62. Luis bought a book and four identical pens for $12. Carlos bought the same book and two similar pens. Carlos paid $4 less than Luis. What was the cost of the book?

63. 250 adults and some children went to the zoo. The admission ticket for each adult was $12 and the admission ticket for each child was $9. If $6,915 was collected for all the tickets, how many children went to the zoo?

64. Mr. Ortiz received a bonus. He gave $2,000 to his wife and distributed an amount of money equally among his six children. He was left with $1,350, which was $400 more than the amount of money he gave to each child. How much was his bonus?

Unit 4: LINE GRAPHS AND TABLES

Example:

The line graph shows the number of gold, silver, and bronze medals given out during an international sports meet.

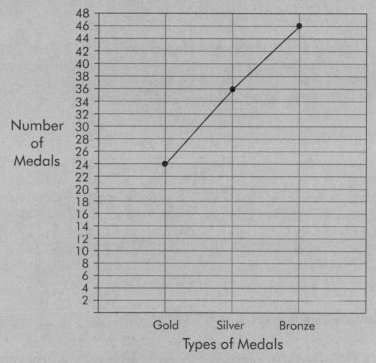

1. How many gold medals were given out?

   24

2. How many silver and bronze medals were given out?

   36 + 46 = **82** silver and bronze medals

3. How many more bronze than gold medals were given out?

   46 − 24 = **22** more bronze medals

4. If there were 58 participants who did not receive any medals, how many participants were there altogether?

   24 + 36 + 46 + 58 = **164** participants

Singapore Math Practice Level 4A

Study the table below and answer questions 1 to 5.

The table shows the number of animals Mario saw in a park.

Animals	Spider	Bird	Cat	Worm
Number of animals	8	?	3	8

1. If there were 30 animals in the park, how many birds were there?

    _____

2. Which animal did Mario see the most in the park?   _____

3. Which animal did Mario see the least in the park?   _____

4. How many more birds than worms did Mario see?   _____

5. If 3 birds, 5 worms, and 4 spiders left the park, how many animals remained in the park?

    _____

Study the data below and answer questions 6 to 11.

Mr. Cox recorded the number of mobile phones he sold over five months in the table below.

November	⊮ ⊮ ⊮ ⊮ ⊮ ⊮ ⊮ ⊮ ⊮ ⊮ ⊮ ⊮ ⊮
December	⊮ ⊮ ⊮ ⊮ ⊮ ⊮
January	⊮ ⊮ ⊮ ⊮ ⊮ ⊮ ⊮ ⊮ ⊮ ⊮ ⊮ ⊮ ⊮ ⊮ ⊮ ⊮ ⊮ ⊮
February	⊮ ⊮ ⊮ ⊮ ⊮ ⊮ ⊮ ⊮ ⊮ ⊮ ⊮
March	⊮ ⊮ ⊮ ⊮ ⊮ ⊮ ⊮ ⊮ ⊮

Singapore Math Practice Level 4A

6. Complete the table below using the above data.

Months	Number of mobile phones sold
November	
December	
January	
February	
March	

7. In which month did Mr. Cox sell the most number of mobile phones?

_____

8. How many more mobile phones did Mr. Cox sell in February than in December?

_____

9. How many mobile phones were sold altogether in the two months with the highest sales?

_____

10. If the number of mobile phones sold in April was twice as many as those sold in March, how many mobile phones were sold in April?

_____

11. If each mobile phone was sold for $102, how much money did Mr. Cox make in February and March?

_____

Singapore Math Practice Level 4A

Study the line graph below and answer questions 12 to 16.

The line graph shows the number of students taking the school bus over a few years.

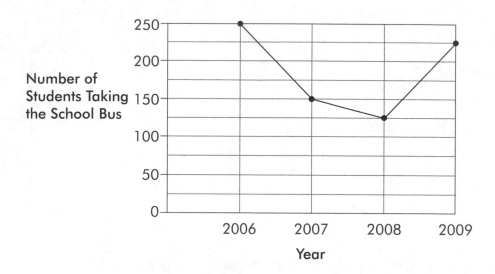

12. How many students took the school bus in 2007? _____

13. In which year was the number of students taking the school bus the greatest?

_____

14. What was the increase in the number of students taking the school bus from 2008 to 2009?

_____

15. What was the difference between the year with the greatest number of students taking the school bus and the year with the lowest number of students taking the school bus?

_____

16. How many students took the school bus from 2006 to 2009?

_____

Study the bar graph below and answer questions 17 to 22.

The bar graph shows the amount of money collected by six children in a donation drive.

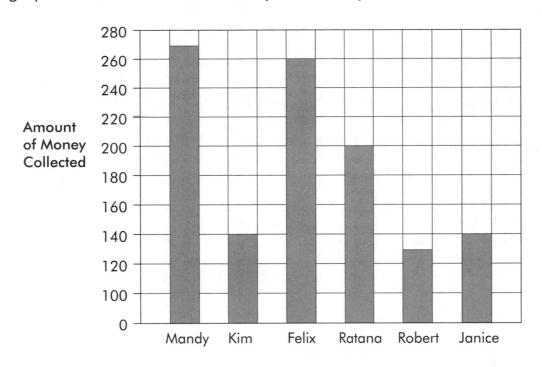

17. Using the data from the bar graph, complete the table below.

Name	Amount of money collected
Mandy	
Kim	
Felix	
Ratana	
Robert	
Janice	

18. Who collected more than $200? _____

19. Which two children collected the same amount of money? _____

20. Who collected twice as much money as Robert? _____

21. How much money was collected altogether? _____

Singapore Math Practice Level 4A

22. How much more money did the children have to collect in order to reach $2,000?

_____

Study the line graph below and answer questions 23 to 27.

The line graph shows the number of visitors to the science center in a month.

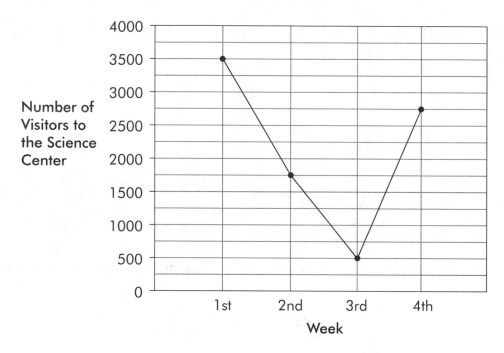

23. In which week was the number of visitors the least?

_____

24. What was the increase in the number of visitors from the 3rd to the 4th week?

_____

25. What was the decrease in the number of visitors from the 1st to the 2nd week?

_____

26. What was the difference in the week with the greatest number of visitors and the week with the lowest number of visitors?

_____

27. If each admission ticket cost $9, how much did the science center collect during the four weeks?

_____

Singapore Math Practice Level 4A

REVIEW 2

Choose the correct answer. Write its number in the parentheses.

1. The product of 943 and 57 is _____.

    (1) 886   (3) 53,175
    (2) 1,000   (4) 53,751   (   )

2. The quotient of 7,256 ÷ 10 is _____.

    (1) 6   (3) 72
    (2) 56   (4) 725   (   )

The table shows the heights of four boys. Study the table below and answer questions 3 and 4.

Name	Height
Hakeem	140 cm
Salim	?
Colin	142 cm
Derrick	136 cm

3. If the total height of the four boys is 557 cm, what is Salim's height?

    (1) 138 cm   (3) 140 cm
    (2) 139 cm   (4) 141 cm   (   )

4. What is the difference between Salim's height and Derrick's height?

    (1) 2 cm   (3) 4 cm
    (2) 3 cm   (4) 6 cm   (   )

Singapore Math Practice Level 4A

The line graph shows Felicia's test scores in mathematics from February to May. Study the line graph and answer questions 5 to 7.

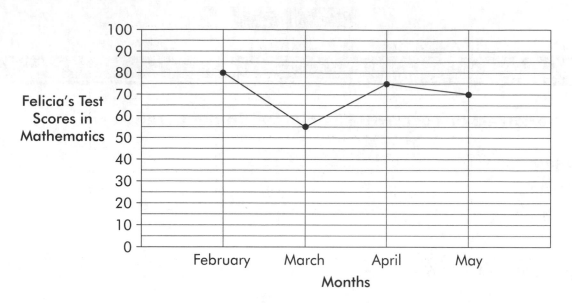

5. What was Felicia's test score in mathematics in March?

    (1) 65   (3) 55

    (2) 60   (4) 50   (   )

6. What was the difference between Felicia's test scores in mathematics in February and in May?

    (1) 5   (3) 15

    (2) 10   (4) 20   (   )

7. In which month did Felicia score the highest in mathematics?

    (1) February   (3) April

    (2) March   (4) May   (   )

Write your answers on the lines.

8. When a number is divided by 8, the answer is 52. What is the number?   _____

9. Estimate the value of 1,785 × 3.   _____

10. 6,123 ÷ 4 = ☐   _____

Singapore Math Practice Level 4A

The table shows the number of stamps and coins Dora collected from four different countries. Study the table below and answer questions 11 to 13.

Country	Stamps	Coins
Malaysia	394	127
Indonesia	?	245
Thailand	125	169
Philippines	178	88

11. If Dora collected a total of 947 stamps, how many Indonesian stamps did she collect?

   _____

12. What was the total number of coins collected by Dora?   _____

13. How many more stamps than coins did Dora collect?   _____

14.   2 0 5
        ×   8 3
     _____

15. $8\overline{)7{,}9\,1\,6}$

Singapore Math Practice Level 4A

Solve the following story problems. Show your work in the space below.

16. Mrs. Kim bought two boxes of pens. Both boxes contained a total of 900 pens. The bigger box contained 120 more pens than the other one. How many pens were in the smaller box?

17. Mr. Santiago bought 36 bicycles, each at $159. He sold all of them for $8,000. How much money did he earn?

18. Tai has 1,230 beads. He has three times as many beads as Reta. Veronica has half as many beads as Reta. How many beads do the three children have altogether?

Singapore Math Practice Level 4A

19. A publisher printed 3,000 books. 54 books were found defective and thrown away, and the rest were sold at $9 each. How much money did the publisher make from the sale of the books?

20. A factory makes 1,395 remote-controlled cars in a week.

   (a)   How many remote-controlled cars can the factory make in eight weeks?

   (b)   If the factory needs to make 40,455 remote-controlled cars in nine weeks, how many remote-controlled cars must the factory make in a week?

Unit 5: FRACTIONS

Examples:

1. Convert $\frac{16}{7}$ into a mixed number.

$$\frac{16}{7} = \frac{14}{7} + \frac{2}{7} = 2 + \frac{2}{7} = \mathbf{2\frac{2}{7}}$$

2. Convert $4\frac{5}{9}$ into an improper fraction.

$$4\frac{5}{9} = \frac{36}{9} + \frac{5}{9} = \frac{\mathbf{41}}{\mathbf{9}}$$

3. What is the sum of $\frac{2}{3}$ and $\frac{8}{9}$? Write your answer in its simplest form.

$$\frac{2^{\times 3}}{3^{\times 3}} + \frac{8}{9} = \frac{6}{9} + \frac{8}{9} = \frac{14}{9} = \mathbf{1\frac{5}{9}}$$

4. Find the value of $\frac{1}{3}$ of 72.

$$\frac{1}{\underset{1}{3}} \times \overset{24}{\cancel{72}} = \underline{\mathbf{24}}$$

Write the correct mixed number on the lines.

1. $3 + \frac{1}{2} =$ _____

2. $6 + \frac{2}{3} =$ _____

3. $5 + \frac{1}{4} =$ _____

4. $9 + \frac{1}{12} =$ _____

Singapore Math Practice Level 4A

5. $7 + \dfrac{5}{7} =$ _____

6. $\dfrac{5}{8} + 4 =$ _____

7. $\dfrac{4}{9} + 1 =$ _____

8. $\dfrac{3}{5} + 2 =$ _____

9. $\dfrac{1}{6} + 8 =$ _____

10. $\dfrac{9}{11} + 3 =$ _____

Fill in each blank with the correct answer.

11.

_____ wholes and _____ fifths = _____

12.

_____ wholes and _____ sevenths = _____

13.

_____ wholes and _____ eighths = _____

14.

_____ wholes and _____ sixth = _____

15.

_____ wholes and _____ twelfths = _____

Singapore Math Practice Level 4A

For each number line, write the correct mixed number in each box.

16.

17.

18.

Fill in each blank with the correct answer.

19. $2 =$ _____ halves

20. $3\frac{1}{3} =$ _____ thirds

21. $5\frac{7}{11} =$ _____ elevenths

22. $1\frac{9}{12} =$ _____ twelfths

23. $8\frac{5}{7} =$ _____ sevenths

24. There are _____ quarters in $4\frac{3}{4}$.

25. There are _____ sixths in $1\frac{5}{6}$.

26. There are _____ eighths in $9\frac{3}{8}$.

27. There are _____ tenths in $6\frac{7}{10}$.

Singapore Math Practice Level 4A

For each number line, write the correct improper fraction in each box. Write each improper fraction in its simplest form.

28.

29.

30.

Write each mixed number as an improper fraction.

31. $1\frac{1}{2} =$

32. $1\frac{3}{10} =$

33. $2\frac{3}{4} =$

34. $4\frac{3}{5} =$

35. $7\frac{1}{6} =$

36. $8\frac{2}{3} =$

37. $3\frac{5}{8} =$

38. $3\frac{7}{12} =$

39. $8\frac{4}{9} =$

40. $2\frac{4}{7} =$

Write each improper fraction as a mixed number.

41. $\frac{11}{2} =$

42. $\frac{9}{4} =$

43. $\frac{5}{5} =$

44. $\frac{16}{2} =$

Singapore Math Practice Level 4A

45. $\dfrac{37}{5} =$

46. $\dfrac{12}{3} =$

47. $\dfrac{15}{8} =$

48. $\dfrac{17}{6} =$

49. $\dfrac{23}{6} =$

50. $\dfrac{38}{9} =$

Add these fractions. Write each answer in its simplest form.

51. $\dfrac{2}{5} + \dfrac{4}{5} =$

52. $\dfrac{2}{3} + \dfrac{4}{9} =$

53. $\dfrac{3}{7} + \dfrac{13}{14} =$

54. $\dfrac{5}{8} + \dfrac{3}{4} =$

55. $\dfrac{7}{12} + \dfrac{2}{6} + \dfrac{9}{12} =$

56. $\dfrac{1}{2} + \dfrac{3}{10} + \dfrac{9}{10} =$

57. $\dfrac{2}{4} + \dfrac{7}{8} + \dfrac{1}{4} =$

58. $\dfrac{1}{3} + \dfrac{3}{9} + \dfrac{5}{9} =$

Subtract these fractions. Write each answer in its simplest form.

59. $6 - \dfrac{2}{8} =$

60. $10 - \dfrac{5}{12} =$

61. $\dfrac{8}{9} - \dfrac{2}{9} =$

62. $\dfrac{9}{10} - \dfrac{1}{2} =$

63. $2\dfrac{6}{9} - \dfrac{1}{3} =$

64. $4\dfrac{9}{12} - \dfrac{2}{4} =$

65. $5\dfrac{7}{12} - \dfrac{1}{4} =$

66. $7 - \dfrac{9}{10} - \dfrac{2}{5} =$

Solve the problems below.

67. $\frac{2}{3}$ of 21 =

68. $\frac{1}{8}$ of 72 =

69. $\frac{5}{9}$ of 81 =

70. $\frac{4}{5}$ of 65 =

71. $\frac{9}{10}$ of 20 =

72. $\frac{5}{6} \times 48 =$

73. $\frac{3}{7} \times 63 =$

74. $\frac{3}{4} \times 52 =$

75. $\frac{4}{9} \times 27 =$

76. $\frac{1}{6} \times 84 =$

Solve the following story problems. Show your work in the space below.

77. Judi baked a cake. She gave $\frac{3}{8}$ of it to her neighbor. What fraction of the cake did she have left?

78. An empty can has a mass of $\frac{1}{6}$ lb. When it is filled with sand, it has a mass of $\frac{7}{12}$ lb. Find the mass of the sand in the can.

Singapore Math Practice Level 4A

79. What is the total mass of three boxes if Box A has a mass of $\frac{5}{6}$ kg, Box B has a mass of $\frac{1}{10}$ kg, and Box C has a mass of $\frac{9}{10}$ kg?

80. After cutting a length of ribbon and giving $\frac{5}{12}$ m of ribbon to her daughter, Mrs. Kwan had $\frac{1}{4}$ m of ribbon left. If she had $\frac{11}{12}$ m of ribbon in the beginning, what was the length of ribbon Mrs. Kwan cut?

81. Maggie, Joyce, and Lina each prepared different amounts of fruit punch for a party. Maggie prepared $\frac{5}{9}$ L of fruit punch and Joyce prepared $\frac{1}{3}$ L of fruit punch. If they had prepared a total of $1\frac{2}{3}$ L of fruit punch, how much fruit punch did Lina prepare?

82. Eduardo drank $\frac{6}{10}$ L of milk. Viktor drank $\frac{1}{2}$ L of milk less than Eduardo. How much milk did the two children drink in all?

83. Mrs. Nguyen bought 5 L of cooking oil. She used $\frac{1}{4}$ L of cooking oil on Monday. She used $\frac{1}{8}$ L of cooking oil on Tuesday. How much cooking oil did she have left?

84. In a race, Carla ran $\frac{3}{4}$ km and swam $\frac{3}{8}$ km. She biked the rest of the race. If she traveled $12\frac{7}{8}$ km altogether, how far did she bike?

Singapore Math Practice Level 4A

85. There are 16 red beads, 24 green beads, and 20 blue beads in a box. What fraction of the beads in the box are blue?

86. The distance from Town A to Town B is 18 miles. Luke starts his journey from Town A and travels $\frac{1}{6}$ of the total distance. How much further does he have to travel in order to reach Town B?

87. There were 32 chocolates in a box. After eating some chocolates, Tara found that she had $\frac{5}{8}$ of the chocolates left. How many chocolates did Tara eat?

88. Farmer Bill had 28 chickens, 15 ducks, and 7 turkeys. He sold $\frac{4}{5}$ of the birds.

    (a) How many birds did he sell in all?

    (b) If he sold 12 chickens, what fraction of the chickens were left?

89. 568 people watched a concert. $\frac{5}{8}$ of the audience were women, while $\frac{1}{4}$ of them were men. How many children were there at the concert?

90. Isabel received a sum of money. She gave $\frac{1}{3}$ of the money to her brother. If she had $60 left, how much money did Isabel receive?

Singapore Math Practice Level 4A

Unit 6: ANGLES

Examples:

1. Draw an angle equal to 135°.

2. Rebeca is playing a game. She stands in the middle of a room.

(a) Rebeca is facing northwest. What can she see?

<u>**laptop**</u>

(b) Rebeca is facing south. If she turns 90° counterclockwise, what will she see?

<u>**chocolates**</u>

(c) Rebeca will see the flowers if she turns 180° clockwise. In which direction is Rebeca facing?

<u>**southwest**</u>

(d) Rebeca is looking at the papers. If she turns **315°** counterclockwise, she will see the radio.

Singapore Math Practice Level 4A

Name the marked angles in another way.

1.

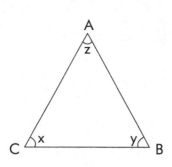

∠ABC = _____

∠ACB = _____

∠BAC = _____

2.

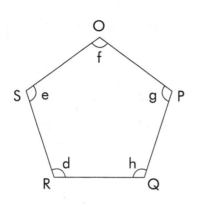

∠d = _____

∠e = _____

∠f = _____

∠g = _____

∠h = _____

Study the following angles and answer questions 3 and 4.

3. Identify the angles that are greater than 90°. _____

4. Identify the angles that are smaller than 90°. _____

Singapore Math Practice Level 4A

Estimate and measure the marked angles with a protractor.

<u>Estimated value</u>   <u>Actual measurement</u>

5.

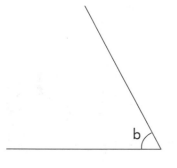

$\angle a = \underline{\quad}°$ $\angle a = \underline{\quad}°$

6.

$\angle b = \underline{\quad}°$ $\angle b = \underline{\quad}°$

7.

$\angle PQR = \underline{\quad}°$ $\angle PQR = \underline{\quad}°$

8.

$\angle XWY = \underline{\quad}°$ $\angle XWY = \underline{\quad}°$

Singapore Math Practice Level 4A

Draw the following angles in the space below.

9. $\angle p = 75°$

10. $\angle r = 108°$

11. $\angle q = 45°$

12. $\angle s = 134°$

Singapore Math Practice Level 4A

Fill in each blank with the correct answer.

13. A _____-turn equals 1 right angle.

14. A half-turn equals _____°.

15. A _____-turn equals 270°.

16. A complete turn equals _____ right angles.

17. _____ of a complete turn is 180°.

18. _____ of a complete turn is 90°.

19. Which direction is each child from X?

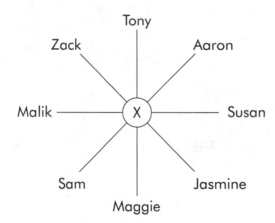

Tony: _____

Aaron: _____

Susan: _____

Jasmine: _____

Maggie: _____

Sam: _____

Malik: _____

Zack: _____

Singapore Math Practice Level 4A

Look at each picture carefully and fill in each blank with the correct answer.

20.

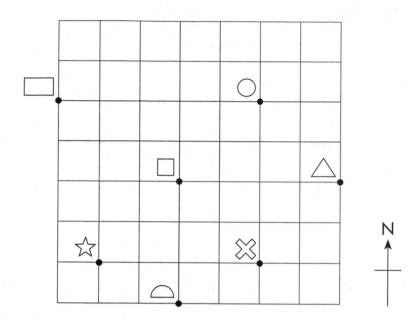

(a)   The circle is _____ of the triangle.

(b)   The semicircle is _____ of the star.

(c)   The square is _____ of the triangle.

(d)   The cross is _____ of the star.

(e)   The square is _____ of the semicircle.

(f)   The circle is _____ of the rectangle.

(g)   The triangle is _____ of the cross.

(h)   The star is _____ of the circle.

21.

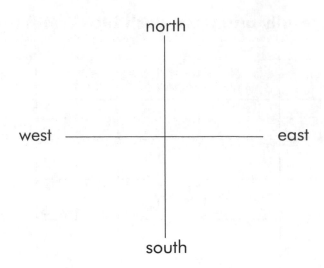

(a)   George is facing north. If he turns clockwise _____°, he will face southwest.

(b)   George is facing west. If he turns counterclockwise _____°, he will face east.

(c)   George is facing northwest. If he turns counterclockwise _____°, he will face northeast.

(d)   George is facing south. If he turns counterclockwise _____° , he will face southeast.

(e)   George is facing east. If he makes a _____-turn clockwise, he will face south.

(f)   George is facing north. If he makes a _____-turn counterclockwise, he will face east.

Singapore Math Practice Level 4A

REVIEW 3

Choose the correct answer. Write its number in the parentheses.

1. Express $6\frac{7}{9}$ as an improper fraction.

    (1) $\frac{22}{9}$ (3) $\frac{61}{9}$

    (2) $\frac{54}{9}$ (4) $\frac{67}{9}$ (   )

2. What is the difference between $\frac{2}{5}$ and $\frac{3}{10}$?

    (1) $\frac{3}{5}$ (3) $\frac{1}{5}$

    (2) $\frac{1}{2}$ (4) $\frac{1}{10}$ (   )

3. $\frac{4}{9} + \frac{2}{3} = $ _____

    (1) $\frac{2}{3}$ (3) $\frac{6}{9}$

    (2) $\frac{2}{9}$ (4) $1\frac{1}{9}$ (   )

4. What fraction of the figure below is shaded?

    (1) $\frac{1}{3}$ (3) $\frac{1}{2}$

    (2) $\frac{5}{12}$ (4) $\frac{7}{12}$ (   )

Singapore Math Practice Level 4A

5. $\frac{2}{7}$ of 98 = _____

    (1)   28   (3)   196
    (2)   49   (4)   343   (   )

6. How many sixths are there in $5\frac{1}{6}$?

    (1)   3   (3)   31
    (2)   12   (4)   57   (   )

7. Measure ∠a.

    (1)   10°   (3)   18°
    (2)   15°   (4)   20°   (   )

Write your answers on the lines.

8.

    31   32   [   ]   33

    What is the missing fraction in the box? Write your answer in its simplest form.

    _____

9. Write $\frac{24}{5}$ as a mixed number in its simplest form.   _____

10. [   ] of a complete turn is 270°.   _____

11. Mrs. Diaz baked a cake. She gave $\frac{1}{2}$ of the cake to her sister and her children ate $\frac{3}{8}$ of the
    cake. How much cake did she have left?

    _____

Singapore Math Practice Level 4A

12. Name the angle marked a in another way.

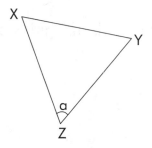

_____

13. Mr. Yang bought 25 bottles of milk. If each bottle contained $\frac{3}{4}$ L of milk, how much milk did Mr. Yang buy?

_____

14. Eight children are standing in different positions shown below. Identify the person who is standing in the northwest.

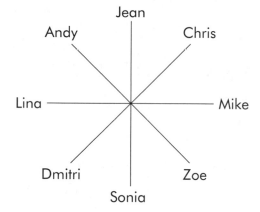

_____

15. Giselle is facing south. If she makes a [   ]° turn in the counterclockwise direction, she will face northeast.

_____

Solve the following story problems. Show your work in the space below.

16. There were 32 children at a party. There were 8 more boys than girls. If 8 girls wore glasses, what fraction of the girls wore glasses at the party?

17. There were 104 people at a museum. $\frac{3}{8}$ of the people were women. If there were 28 children at the museum, how many men were there?

18. Ana had some money. She used $\frac{4}{7}$ of it to buy a pair of shoes which cost $96. If she spent another $\frac{2}{7}$ of the money to buy a dress, how much did she spend altogether?

70

19. Draw an angle of 168° and label it as x.

Look at the picture and fill in each blank with the correct answer.

20.

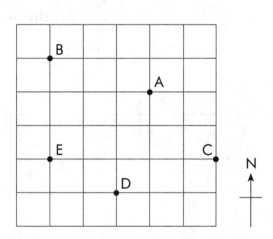

(a)   Letter A is _____ of letter B.

(b)   Letter B is _____ of letter E.

(c)   Letter C is _____ of letter D.

(d)   Letter E is _____ of letter D.

(e)   Letter E is _____ of letter C.

Unit 7: PERPENDICULAR AND PARALLEL LINES

Examples:

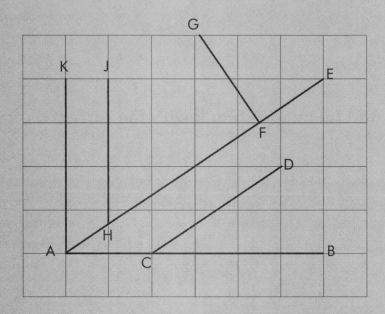

1. Identify all the perpendicular lines.

    <u>KA ⊥ AB</u> and <u>GF ⊥ HE</u>

2. Identify all the parallel lines.

    <u>HE // CD</u> and <u>KA // JH</u>

3. Identify all vertical lines.

    <u>KA</u> and <u>JH</u>

4. Identify all horizontal lines.

    <u>AB</u>

Singapore Math Practice Level 4A

1. Draw a line perpendicular to the line AB through the point Z.

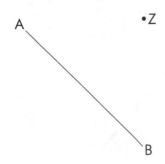

2. Draw a line perpendicular to the line CD through the point Y.

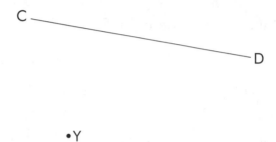

3. (a) Draw a line perpendicular to the line EF through the point X.

    (b) Draw a line perpendicular to the line EF through the point Y.

Singapore Math Practice Level 4A

4. (a) Draw a line perpendicular to line GH through the point A.

    (b) Draw a line perpendicular to line GH through the point B.

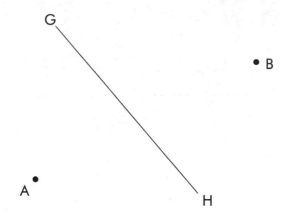

5. Draw a line parallel to MN through the point S.

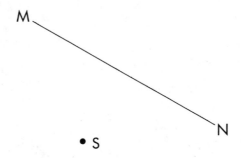

6. Draw a pair of parallel lines through the points V and W.

• V

• W

Singapore Math Practice Level 4A

7. (a) Draw a line parallel to AB through the point X.

    (b) Draw a line parallel to AB through the point Y.

8.

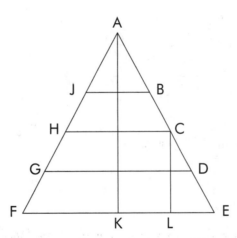

    (a) Identify all pairs of parallel lines in the figure above.

    (b) Identify all pairs of perpendicular lines in the figure above.

9. The figure below shows a section of a brick wall.

   (a) Draw a vertical line through A to meet XY and label it as AB.

   (b) Draw a horizontal line through A and label it as AC.

10. The figure below shows a rectangular fish tank.

   (a) Identify all the horizontal lines.   _____

   (b) Identify all the vertical lines.   _____

11. The figure on the right shows a box.

   (a) Line AB is a _____ line.

   (b) Line BC is a _____ line.

   (c) Line DC is a _____ line.

   (d) Line AD is a _____ line.

Singapore Math Practice Level 4A

Examples:

1. Is this figure a rectangle or a square? List one property.

   This figure is a square.

   It has four sides. / All four sides are equal. / It has two pairs of parallel lines. / All four angles are right angles.

2. The figure below is made up of a rectangle and a square.

   (a) Find the length of AG.

   (b) Find the length of CE.

   (a) FE = 22 cm

      AG = 39 − 22 = <u>17 cm</u>

   (b) CE = 13 + 22 = <u>35 cm</u>

Look at the figures below.

1. (a) Is Figure A a rectangle or a square? _____

   (b) State two properties of Figure A.

   _____

   _____

2. (a) Is Figure B a rectangle or a square? _____

   (b) State two properties of Figure B.

   _____

   _____

3. (a) Is Figure C a rectangle or a square? _____

   (b) State two properties of Figure C.

   _____

   _____

4. Draw Figure X in the box based on the given hints.

- It has four equal sides.
- It has two pairs of parallel lines.
- It has four right angles.

5. Draw Figure Z in the box based on the given hints.

- It has four sides.
- It has two pairs of parallel lines.
- It has equal opposite sides.

6. Find the unknown sides.

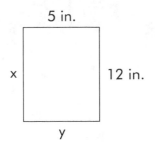

x = _____ in.

y = _____ in.

Singapore Math Practice Level 4A

7. If the length of the figure below is five times its width, find the unknown sides.

40 cm

x

y

x = _____ cm

y = _____ cm

8. Find the unknown sides.

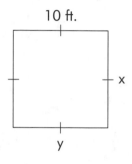

10 ft.

x

y

x = _____ ft.

y = _____ ft.

9. The figure below is not drawn to scale. Find the unknown marked angle.

z

15°

$\angle z$ = _____ °

10. The figure below is not drawn to scale. Find the unknown marked angle.

z   18°

25°

$\angle z$ = _____ °

Singapore Math Practice Level 4A

11. The figure below is not drawn to scale. Find the unknown marked angle.

$\angle z = $ _____ °

12. The figure below is not drawn to scale. Find the unknown marked angle.

$\angle z = $ _____ °

13. The figure below is not drawn to scale. Find the unknown marked angle.

$\angle z = $ _____ °

Singapore Math Practice Level 4A

14. The figure below is made up of two rectangles. Find AB and AH.

15. The figure below is made up of two identical squares and a rectangle. Find DF and EF.

16. The figure below is made up of three rectangles. Find EF and DE.

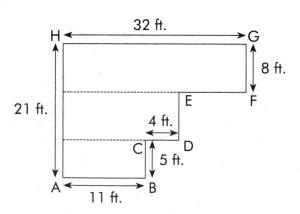

Singapore Math Practice Level 4A

17. The figure below is made up of a big rectangle and two small identical rectangles. Find ML and AB.

18. The figure below is made up of two rectangles and a square. Find BC and EF.

REVIEW 4

Choose the correct answer. Write its number in the parentheses.

1. Which of the following lines shows a vertical line?

   (1) Line AB   (3) Line EF

   (2) Line CD   (4) Line GH   (   )

2. How many pairs of parallel lines are there in the figure below?

   (1) 2

   (2) 3

   (3) 4

   (4) 5   (   )

3. The figure below shows a rectangle. If the length of the rectangle is 3 cm more than its width, find x.

   (1) 14 cm

   (2) 15 cm

   (3) 18 cm

   (4) 20 cm   (   )

4. The figure below is not drawn to scale. Find the unknown marked angle in the figure below.

   (1) 16°

   (2) 42°

   (3) 64°

   (4) 106°   (   )

84

The figure below is made up of two identical squares and two identical rectangles. Use this figure to answer questions 5 and 6.

5.   Find the length of AJ.

  (1)   12 cm   (3)   24 cm
  (2)   22 cm   (4)   35 cm   (   )

6.   Find the length of FE.

  (1)   35 cm   (3)   11 cm
  (2)   22 cm   (4)   10 cm   (   )

For questions 7 and 8, refer to the figure below.

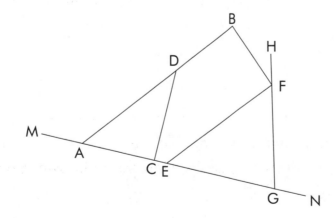

7.   Which line is perpendicular to MN?

  (1)   BA   (3)   FE
  (2)   DC   (4)   HG   (   )

Singapore Math Practice Level 4A

8. Which line is parallel to AB?

   (1) BF   (3) EF
   (2) CD   (4) GH   (   )

9. How many lines are parallel to Line XY in the figure below?

   (1) 2
   (2) 3
   (3) 4
   (4) 5   (   )

10. How many horizontal lines are there in the figure below?

   (1) 2
   (2) 3
   (3) 4
   (4) 6   (   )

Write your answers on the lines.

11. Identify a line perpendicular to line XY.

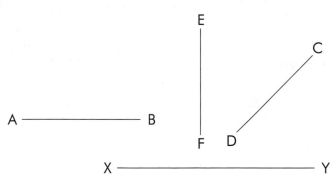

                                                    _____

12. The figure below is not drawn to scale. Find the unknown marked angle.

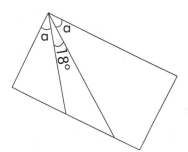

                                                    _____

86

13. State one property of the figure shown below.

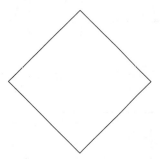

_____

14. The figure below is made up of two identical rectangles. Find line AF.

_____

15. Identify two parallel lines in the figure shown below.

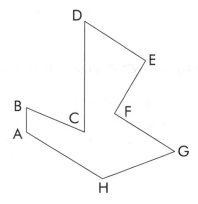

_____

Use the following figure to answer questions 16 and 17.

16. (a) AF and BE are _____ lines.

    (b) AB and FE are _____ lines.

17. (a) What type of line is GD?   _____

    (b) What type of line is BC?   _____

18.

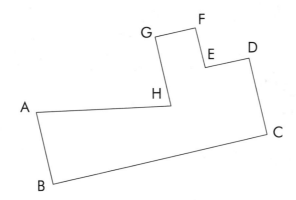

The line perpendicular to line DC in the above figure is line _____.

Singapore Math Practice Level 4A

19.   Draw a figure based on the given hints.

  •   It has two pairs of parallel lines.

  •   It has four sides.

20.   Draw a line that is parallel to GH.

Singapore Math Practice Level 4A

FINAL REVIEW

Choose the correct answer. Write its number in the parentheses.

1. 1,500 more than 86,576 is _____.

    (1) 85,026   (3) 87,581

    (2) 85,076   (4) 88,076   (   )

2. The digit 0 in 13,095 is in the _____ place.

    (1) ten thousands   (3) hundreds

    (2) thousands   (4) tens   (   )

3. Forty-five thousand, forty written in numeral is _____.

    (1) 45,014   (3) 45,140

    (2) 45,040   (4) 45,400   (   )

4. Which of the following is **not** a factor of 66?

    (1) 2   (3) 8

    (2) 3   (4) 11   (   )

5. Which of the following is 9,000 when rounded to the nearest ten?

    (1) 8,990   (3) 9,004

    (2) 8,994   (4) 9,009   (   )

6. $3\frac{2}{5} = \frac{\square}{5}$. The missing number in the box is _____.

    (1) 7   (3) 15

    (2) 10   (4) 17   (   )

Singapore Math Practice Level 4A

7. 3,904 × 8 = _____
   (1) 30,232   (3) 31,520
   (2) 31,232   (4) 32,520   (   )

8. How many quarters are there in $5\frac{3}{4}$?
   (1) 15   (3) 20
   (2) 19   (4) 23   (   )

9. A movie theater sold 1,659 tickets on Thursday and three times as many tickets on Friday. How many tickets did it sell on both days?
   (1) 3,318   (3) 6,636
   (2) 4,977   (4) 8,295   (   )

10. Anya spent $40 and had $10 left. What fraction of her money did she spend?
   (1) $\frac{1}{5}$ (3) $\frac{3}{4}$
   (2) $\frac{1}{4}$ (4) $\frac{4}{5}$ (   )

The following table shows Lily's grades in four subjects. Study it carefully and answer questions 11 and 12.

Subject	English	Math	Science	Social studies
Grade	75	90	63	81

11. What was the total score for Lily's best three subjects?
   (1) 219   (3) 234
   (2) 228   (4) 246   (   )

12. What was the difference between the highest and the lowest scores?
   (1) 9   (3) 18
   (2) 15   (4) 27   (   )

Singapore Math Practice Level 4A

13. How many pair(s) of perpendicular lines are in the figure below?

    (1) 1
    (2) 2
    (3) 3
    (4) 4

    (　　)

14. Charlotte is facing north. If she turns counterclockwise 225°, she will be facing _____.

    (1) northeast   (3) northwest
    (2) southeast   (4) southwest   (　　)

15. Find ∠m with the use of a protractor.

    (1) 55°
    (2) 60°
    (3) 115°
    (4) 120°

    (　　)

16. Which of the following is the third multiple of 8?

    (1) 16   (3) 26
    (2) 24   (4) 28   (　　)

17. The figure below is made up of a rectangle and a square. Find QR.

    (1) 10 yd.
    (2) 12 yd.
    (3) 15 yd.
    (4) 18 yd.

    (　　)

Singapore Math Practice Level 4A

18. 14 thousands more than 58,750 is _____.

    (1)   44,750   (3)   58,764

    (2)   58,736   (4)   72,750   (   )

19. $1,489 \div 8 =$ _____ R _____

    (1)   185, 1   (3)   186, 1

    (2)   185, 6   (4)   186, 5   (   )

20. Which of the following shows an angle of 85°?

    (1)   (3)

    (2)   (4)

                                                      (   )

Write your answers on the lines.

21. 2 ten thousands + 5 thousands + 31 hundreds + 6 tens + 4 ones = ⬜

    Write the correct answer in numeral.   _____

22. Complete the number pattern.

    35,070, ⬜ , 35,230, 35,310, 35,390   _____

23. 180° = ⬜ –turn   _____

24. Find the product of 532 and 37.   _____

25. 21 and 42 are the first two common multiples of ⬜ and ⬜ .

                                                      _____

26. Write $\frac{58}{6}$ as a mixed number in its simplest form. _____

27. Measure ∠x.

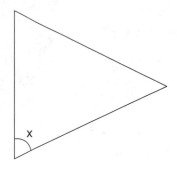

_____

28. Draw a line perpendicular to CD through the point X.

•X

C ———————————
                    ———— D

29. WXYZ is a square. It is not drawn to scale. Find ∠a and ∠b.

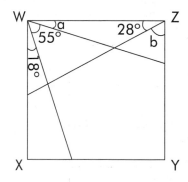

∠a = _____

∠b = _____

30. Find the value of $3 + \frac{2}{5} + \frac{9}{10}$. _____

Singapore Math Practice Level 4A

31. Based on the given hints, write 'Nicholas' and 'Zoe' in the correct boxes.

- Nicholas is standing north of Susie.
- Zoe is standing southwest of Susie.

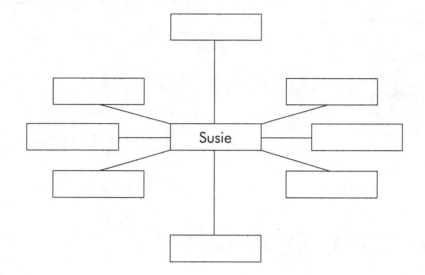

32. Fill in each box with the correct answer.

$$0 \quad \frac{1}{10} \quad \frac{1}{5} \quad \frac{3}{10} \quad \boxed{} \quad \frac{1}{2} \quad \frac{3}{5} \quad \boxed{} \quad \frac{4}{5} \quad \boxed{} \quad 1$$

For questions 33 and 34, study the table below. It shows the number of pots of flowers sold by a florist during a five-day fair.

Monday	ЖҐ ЖҐ ЖҐ I
Tuesday	ЖҐ ЖҐ II
Wednesday	ЖҐ ЖҐ ЖҐ III
Thursday	ЖҐ ЖҐ ЖҐ ЖҐ
Friday	ЖҐ ЖҐ ЖҐ ЖҐ IIII

Singapore Math Practice Level 4A

33. Use the data from the previous table to complete the following table.

Day	Number of pots of flowers
Monday	
Tuesday	
Wednesday	
Thursday	
Friday	

34. How many pots of flowers did the florist sell in all? _____

35. Estimate the value of 421 ÷ 8. _____

36. How many right angles are there in the figure below?

_____

37. When a number is divided by 7, it has a quotient of 26 and a remainder of 5. What is the number?

_____

38. Mrs. Takashi bought 12 lb. of flour. She used $\frac{5}{6}$ of it to bake some pies. How much flour does she have left?

_____

39. $9,055 \times 7 \approx$ ☐ _____

Singapore Math Practice Level 4A

40. Draw an angle measuring 270°.

Solve the following story problems. Show your work in the space below.

41. Mr. Fay saved $630 a month for eight months. He then bought a television set and a stereo. After paying $295 for the stereo, he had $1,853 left. What was the cost of the television set?

42. A soccer ball costs $15 more than a book. A remote-controlled car costs $198 more than the soccer ball. If the remote-controlled car costs $230, what is the cost of the book?

43. Alex, Juan, and Cindy shared a pizza. Alex ate $\frac{1}{4}$ of it. Brandon ate $\frac{1}{8}$ of the pizza more than Alex, and Cindy ate the rest of the pizza. What fraction of the pizza did Cindy eat?

44. Esther had 56 stickers. She gave $\frac{3}{8}$ of them to her sister. She gave some stickers to her friend. If she had 18 stickers left, how many stickers did she give to her friend?

45. Mr. Popovic is 76 years old and his granddaughter is 12 years old this year. In how many years will Mr. Popovic be five times as old as his granddaughter?

CHALLENGE QUESTIONS

Solve the following questions on another sheet of paper.

1. The number of eggs sold by Mrs. Bowles was observed in the pattern shown below.
   Fill in each box with the correct answer.

Day	1	2	3	4	5	6	7	8
Number of eggs sold	15	25		48	61		90	

2. Shani is four times as old as Jenny. Jenny is 3 years older than Enrique. If their total age is 57, how old will Jenny be in four years?

3. When I divide Number A by Number B, the answer is $6\frac{1}{4}$. If Number A is less than 30 and Number B is less than 10, what are numbers A and B?

4. I am a 5-digit number. My first digit is 2 more than the last digit but 2 less than my second digit. My second digit is the third multiple of 3, while my fourth digit is the second multiple of 3. My third digit is the difference between my second and fourth digits. What number am I?

5. The product of numbers X and Y is 600. The sum of the two numbers is 50. What are numbers X and Y?

6. Chet scored six times higher than Hugo on an English test. Jason's score on the same test was the sixth multiple of 10. If the three boys scored a total of 172, what was Chet's score on the test?

7. The difference of two numbers is 132. When one of the numbers is divided by the other, the quotient is 12. What are the two numbers?

8. Mieke wants to buy a bag. She saves $2 the first week. She saves $4 the second week. She saves $6 the third week and so on. In order to buy the bag, she needs to save for 8 weeks at this pattern. How much does the bag cost?

9. I am a 4-digit number. All my digits are factors of 8. The product of the first and last digits is the fourth multiple of 8. The second digit is 3 less than the last digit. If the first digit is the largest number, what number am I?

10. Place the first six multiples of 6 in each box so that the sum of each row is equal to the 10th and 11th multiples of 6.

			10th multiple of 6
			11th multiple of 6

11. Mr. Garza earns twice as much as his wife. Mrs. Garza earns twice as much as her sister. If Mrs. Garza's sister earns $1,255 a month, how much do the three of them earn in a year?

12. The clock below shows the time Sylvia wakes up in the morning. When the minute hand turns 150°, Sylvia eats her breakfast. At what time does Sylvia eat her breakfast?

Singapore Math Practice Level 4A

SOLUTIONS
Singapore Math Practice Level 4A

Unit 1: Whole Numbers (Part 1)

1. twenty-three thousand, seven hundred, one
2. forty thousand, eight hundred, twenty-five
3. sixty-eight thousand, ninety
4. fifty-five thousand, two
5. fourteen thousand, eleven
6. **11,602**
7. **92,314**
8. **57,012**
9. **60,245**
10. **82,001**
11. **6, 20, 300, 5,000, 10,000**
12. **7, 10, 200, 8,000, 50,000**
13. **5, 30, 0, 8,000, 70,000**
14. **0, 20, 400, 1,000, 80,000**
15. **ten thousands**
16. **tens**
17. **8**
18. **0**
19. (a) **80,000/80 thousands**
    (b) **1,000/1 thousand**
    (c) **200/2 hundreds**
    (d) **40/4 tens**
    (e) **6/6 ones**
20. **2**
21. **1**
22. **3**
23. **6**
24. **3,000**
25. **10**
26. **9,000**
27. **100**
28. **80,000**
29. **49,561**
30. **98,075**
31. **13,689**
32. **9,173**
33. **1,359, 1,593, 5,319, 5,931**
34. **12,643, 14,632, 24,163, 41,562**
35. **4,586, 4,685, 6,845, 8,564**
36. **7,410, 7,014, 1,740, 1,407**
37. **96,268, 63,892, 39,628, 26,983**
38. **5,362, 5,236, 3,652, 2,653**
39. **286, 306**
    246 − 126 = 20
    20 + 266 = 286
    20 + 286 = 306
40. **33,055, 33,060**
    33,050 − 33,045 = 5
    5 + 33,050 = 33,055
    5 + 33,055 = 33,060

41. **7,530, 7,560**
    7,550 − 7,540 = 10
    7,540 − 10 = 7,530
    7,550 + 10 = 7,560
42. **90,455, 91,455**
    89,455 − 88,455 = 1,000
    1,000 + 89,455 = 90,455
    1,000 + 90,455 = 91,455
43. **43,012**
    43,112 − 100 = 43,012
44. **94,586**
    94,606 − 20 = 94,586
45. **20,096**
    18,096 + 2,000 = 20,096
46. **81,493**
    80,493 + 1,000 = 81,493
47. **18,475**
    21,475 − 3,000 = 18,475
48. **9,900**
    10,000 − 100 = 9,900
49. **10,381**
    6,000 + 4,381 = 10,381
50. **90,099**
    99 + 90,000 = 90,099

Unit 2: Whole Numbers (Part 2)

1. **770**
2. **850**
3. **660**
4. **300**
5. **1,090**
6. **1,780**
7. **39,920**
8. **46,550**
9. **11,200**
10. **60,000**
11. **500**
12. **900**
13. **3,100**
14. **1,100**
15. **6,900**
16. **89,500**
17. **23,900**
18. **12,100**
19. **61,300**
20. **74,800**
21. **40 + 10 = 50**
22. **670 + 50 = 720**
23. **70 + 730 = 800**
24. **930 − 20 = 910**

25. **420 − 40 = 380**
26. **520 − 20 = 500**
27. **50 × 8 = 400**
28. **30 × 7 = 210**
29. **300 − 10 = 290**
30. **700 − 90 = 610**
31. **120 ÷ 4 = 30**
32. **320 ÷ 5 = 64**
33. **460 + 90 + 550 = 1,100**
34. **880 + 120 + 40 = 1,040**
35. **1, 12**
    2, 6
    3, 4
    1, 2, 3, 4, 6, 12
36. **1, 42**
    2, 21
    3, 14
    6, 7
    1, 2, 3, 6, 7, 14, 21, 42
37. **1, 36**
    2, 18
    3, 12
    4, 9
    6, 6
    1, 2, 3, 4, 6, 9, 12, 18, 36
38. (a) **1, 2, 4, 8**
    (b) **1, 2, 4, 8, 16**
    (c) **1, 2, 4, 8**
39. (a) **1, 2, 7, 14**
    (b) **1, 2, 4, 7, 14, 28**
    (c) **1, 2, 7, 14**
40. (a) **1, 3, 9**
    (b) **1, 2, 3, 6, 9, 18**
    (c) **1, 3, 9**
41. **5, 10, 15, 20**
42. **9, 18, 27**
43. **18**
44. **35**
45. (a) **2, 4, 6, 8, 10, 12**
    (b) **3, 6, 9, 12, 15, 18**
    (c) **6, 12**
46. (a) **4, 8, 12, 16, 20, 24**
    (b) **8, 16, 24, 32, 40, 48**
    (c) **8, 16, 24**
47. 13,800 + 25,300 = **39,100 km**
48. 25,000 − 7,982 = 17,018
    17,018 ≈ **17,020**
49. 1,345 + 7,609 = 8,954
    8,954 ≈ **8,960 books**
50. 1,124 + 259 = 1,383
    1,124 + 1,383 = 2,507
    2,507 ≈ **2,500 students**
51. **10**
    The factors of 10 are 1, 2, 5, and 10.
52. **56**
    56 = 8 × 7
53. **24**
    8 × 3 = 24
    48 = 2 × 24

54. **8**
    32 = 4 × 8
55. **2** and **7**
    2 × 7 = 14
    2 × 14 = 28
    7 × 4 = 28
    The multiples of 2 are 2, 4, 6, 8, 10, 12, ⑭, 16, 18, 20, 22, 24, 26, ㉘, 30, ...
    The multiples of 7 are 7, ⑭, 21, ㉘, 35, ...
    The 2 one-digit numbers are 2 and 7.

Review 1

1. **(1)**
   72,845 is seventy-two thousand, eight hundred, forty-five.
2. **(2)**
   The digit 8 stands for 8,000/8 thousands.
3. **(1)**

18 ÷ 8 = 2 R 2	18 ÷ 6 = 3
24 ÷ 8 = 3	24 ÷ 6 = 4
72 ÷ 8 = 9	72 ÷ 6 = 12
144 ÷ 8 = 18	144 ÷ 6 = 24

   Therefore 18 is not a common multiple of 8 and 6.
4. **(3)**
   1,987 + 5,248 ≈ 1,990 + 5,250 = 7,240
5. **(2)**
   Factors of 28: 1, 2, 4, 7, 14, 28
   Factors of 36: 1, 2, 3, 4, 6, 9, 12, 18, 36
   The common factors of 28 and 36 are 1, 2, and 4.
6. **(3)**
   7,030 − 6,020 = 1,010
   9,050 − 1,010 = 8,040
7. **(1)**
   10,000 − 2,000 = 8,000
   8,000 − 2,000 = 6,000
   2,000 + 1,000 = 3,000
   2,000 + 800 = 2,800
8. **(2)**
   The first four multiples of 7 are 7, 14, 21, and 28.
9. **(3)**
   49,753 = 40,000 + 9,000 + 700 + 50 + 3
   40,000 is 4 ten thousands.
10. **(1)**
    400 × 9 = 3,600
11. **forty-nine thousand, five**
12. **thousands**
13. **15,005, 15,050, 15,500**
14. **1,520**
    559 + 19 + 942 ≈ 560 + 20 + 940 = 1,520
15. **63**
    7 × 9 = 63
16. **89,100**
17. **50,907**
    50,000 + 900 + 7 = 50,907
18. **1, 3, 5, 9, 15, 45**
    1 × 45 = 45
    3 × 15 = 45
    5 × 9 = 45

Singapore Math Practice Level 4A

The factors of 45 are 1, 3, 5, 9, 15, and 45.
19. **0**
    18,360 + 2,598 = 20,958
20. **12** and **24**
    Multiples of 4: 4, 8, ⑫, 16, 20, ㉔, 28, ...
    Multiples of 6: 6, ⑫, 18, ㉔, 30, 36, 42, 48, ...

Unit 3: Whole Numbers (Part 3)

1.
$$\begin{array}{r} 4\,1\,2 \\ \times\quad 4 \\ \hline \mathbf{1,6\,4\,8} \end{array}$$

2.
$$\begin{array}{r} 5\,\overset{1}{4}\,7 \\ \times\quad 2 \\ \hline \mathbf{1,0\,9\,4} \end{array}$$

3.
$$\begin{array}{r} 6\,1\,0 \\ \times\quad 5 \\ \hline \mathbf{3,0\,5\,0} \end{array}$$

4.
$$\begin{array}{r} \overset{1}{9}\,\overset{1}{3}\,5 \\ \times\quad 3 \\ \hline \mathbf{2,8\,0\,5} \end{array}$$

5.
$$\begin{array}{r} 1\,\overset{6}{0}\,9 \\ \times\quad 7 \\ \hline \mathbf{7\,6\,3} \end{array}$$

6.
$$\begin{array}{r} \overset{1}{5},\overset{1}{3}\,\overset{4}{1}\,7 \\ \times\quad 6 \\ \hline \mathbf{3\,1,9\,0\,2} \end{array}$$

7.
$$\begin{array}{r} 2,0\,1\,1 \\ \times\quad 8 \\ \hline \mathbf{1\,6,0\,8\,8} \end{array}$$

8.
$$\begin{array}{r} 6,\overset{2}{0}\,\overset{7}{2}\,8 \\ \times\quad 9 \\ \hline \mathbf{5\,4,2\,5\,2} \end{array}$$

9.
$$\begin{array}{r} \overset{2}{1},\overset{1}{5}\,\overset{3}{2}\,6 \\ \times\quad 5 \\ \hline \mathbf{7,6\,3\,0} \end{array}$$

10.
$$\begin{array}{r} \overset{3}{8},\overset{2}{4}\,\overset{5}{3}\,7 \\ \times\quad 8 \\ \hline \mathbf{6\,7,4\,9\,6} \end{array}$$

11.
$$\begin{array}{r} \overset{4}{4}\,6 \\ \times\quad 1\,8 \\ \hline 3\,6\,8 \\ 4\,6\quad \\ \hline \mathbf{8\,2\,8} \end{array}$$

12.
$$\begin{array}{r} \overset{1}{3}\,5 \\ \times\quad 2\,0 \\ \hline 0\,0 \\ 7\,0\quad \\ \hline \mathbf{7\,0\,0} \end{array}$$

13.
$$\begin{array}{r} \overset{2}{\overset{4}{6}}\,7 \\ \times\quad 3\,6 \\ \hline 4\,0\,2 \\ 2\,0\,1\quad \\ \hline \mathbf{2,4\,1\,2} \end{array}$$

14.
$$\begin{array}{r} 9\,1 \\ \times\quad 2\,7 \\ \hline 6\,3\,7 \\ 1,8\,2\quad \\ \hline \mathbf{2,4\,5\,7} \end{array}$$

15.
$$\begin{array}{r} \overset{5}{8}\,9 \\ \times\quad 1\,6 \\ \hline 5\,3\,4 \\ 8\,9\quad \\ \hline \mathbf{1,4\,2\,4} \end{array}$$

16.
$$\begin{array}{r} \overset{1}{1}\,\overset{3}{2}\,6 \\ \times\quad 5\,0 \\ \hline 0\,0\,0 \\ 6\,3\,0\quad \\ \hline \mathbf{6,3\,0\,0} \end{array}$$

17.
$$\begin{array}{r} \overset{1}{6}\,\overset{3}{2}\,5 \\ \times\quad 7\,3 \\ \hline 1\,8\,7\,5 \\ 4\,3\,7\,5\quad \\ \hline \mathbf{4\,5,6\,2\,5} \end{array}$$

18.
$$\begin{array}{r} 6\,\overset{1}{\overset{3}{1}}\,9 \\ \times\quad 2\,4 \\ \hline 2\,4\,7\,6 \\ 1\,2\,3\,8\quad \\ \hline \mathbf{1\,4,8\,5\,6} \end{array}$$

19.
$$\begin{array}{r} \overset{4}{\overset{2}{2}}\,8\,1 \\ \times\quad 5\,3 \\ \hline 8\,4\,3 \\ 1\,4\,0\,5\quad \\ \hline \mathbf{1\,4,8\,9\,3} \end{array}$$

20.
$$\begin{array}{r} \overset{2}{\overset{4}{3}}\,8\,0 \\ \times\quad 3\,6 \\ \hline 2\,2\,8\,0 \\ 1\,1\,4\,0\quad \\ \hline \mathbf{1\,3,6\,8\,0} \end{array}$$

21.
$$\begin{array}{r} \mathbf{2\,7\,1} \\ 5\,\overline{)\,1,3\,5\,5} \\ 1\,0\quad\quad \\ \hline 3\,5\quad \\ 3\,5\quad \\ \hline 5 \\ 5 \\ \hline 0 \end{array}$$

22.
$$\begin{array}{r} \mathbf{1\,6\,0\,9} \\ 3\,\overline{)\,4,8\,2\,7} \\ 3\quad\quad\quad \\ \hline 1\,8\quad\quad \\ 1\,8\quad\quad \\ \hline 2\quad \\ 0\quad \\ \hline 2\,7 \\ 2\,7 \\ \hline 0 \end{array}$$

23.

```
      4, 9 0 2
  2 ) 9, 8 0 4
      8
      ─
      1 8
      1 8
      ───
          0
          0
          ─
            4
            4
            ─
            0
```

24.

```
        7 6 1
  8 ) 6, 0 8 8
      5 6
      ───
        4 8
        4 8
        ───
          8
          8
          ─
          0
```

25.

```
        2 4 3
  6 ) 1, 4 5 8
      1 2
      ───
        2 5
        2 4
        ───
          1 8
          1 8
          ───
            0
```

26.

```
        3 7 7
  3 ) 1, 1 3 1
      9
      ─
      2 3
      2 1
      ───
        2 1
        2 1
        ───
          0
```

27. 18, 2, 36, 360
28. 69, 4, 276, 2,760
29. 98, 3, 294, 2,940
30. 53, 6, 318, 3,180
31. 77, 9, 693, 6,930
32. 42, 8, 336, 3,360
33 571, 1

```
        5 7 1
  8 ) 4, 5 6 9
      4 0
      ───
        5 6
        5 6
        ───
            9
            8
            ─
            1
```

34. 269, 3

```
        2 6 9
  5 ) 1, 3 4 8
      1 0
      ───
        3 4
        3 0
        ───
          4 8
          4 5
          ───
            3
```

35. 605, 5

```
        6 0 5
  7 ) 4, 2 4 0
      4 2
      ───
          4
          0
          ─
          4 0
          3 5
          ───
            5
```

36. 783, 2

```
        7 8 3
  4 ) 3, 1 3 4
      2 8
      ───
        3 3
        3 2
        ───
          1 4
          1 2
          ───
            2
```

37. 1042, 3

```
      1, 0 4 2
  9 ) 9, 3 8 1
      9
      ─
      3
      0
      ─
      3 8
      3 6
      ───
        2 1
        1 8
        ───
          3
```

38. 60, 20, 1,200
39. 600, 60, 36,000
40. 900, 30, 27,000
41. 240, 48
42. 4,900, 700
43. 8,100, 900

44. (a) 4,368
(b) $80 \times 50 = $ **4,000**
(c) **Yes**

```
          2
        8 4
    ×   5 2
    ─────────
      1 6 8
    4 2 0
    ─────────
    4, 3 6 8
```

45. (a) 38,037
(b) $400 \times 90 = $ **36,000**
(c) **Yes**

```
          8
          2
        4 0 9
    ×     9 3
    ─────────
    1 2 2 7
    3 6 8 1
    ─────────
    3 8, 0 3 7
```

46. (a) 37,088
(b) $1,000 \times 40 = $ **40,000**
(c) **Yes**

```
          2 1
          6 4
        9 7 6
    ×     3 8
    ─────────
    7 8 0 8
    2 9 2 8
    ─────────
    3 7, 0 8 8
```

47. (a) 5 R 3
$43 \div 8 = 5 \text{ R } 3$
(b) $40 \div 8 = $ **5**
(c) **Yes**

48. (a) 89 R 4
(b) $540 \div 6 = $ **90**
(c) **Yes**

```
        8 9
  6 ) 5 3 8
      4 8
      ───
        5 8
        5 4
        ───
          4
```

49. (a) 2,191 R 1
(b) $8,800 \div 4 = $ **2,200**
(c) **Yes**

```
      2, 1 9 1
  4 ) 8, 7 6 5
      8
      ─
      7
      4
      ─
      3 6
      3 6
      ───
          5
          4
          ─
          1
```

50.

$12 \times 255 = 3,060$

```
          1 1
        2 5 5
    ×     1 2
    ─────────
      5 1 0
    2 5 5
    ─────────
    3, 0 6 0
```

There are **3,060** balloons in a dozen packets.

51.

$2,275 \div 7 = 325$
$3 \times 325 = 975$

$$
\begin{array}{r}
325 \\
7\overline{)2,275} \\
21 \\
\hline
17 \\
14 \\
\hline
35 \\
35 \\
\hline
0
\end{array}
$$

$$
\begin{array}{r}
3\overset{1}{2}5 \\
\times \quad 3 \\
\hline
975
\end{array}
$$

It makes **975** watches in 3 days.

52.

| Shirts | $253 | $253 | $253 | $253 | } ? |
| Ties | $78 | $78 | $78 | | |

$4 \times \$253 = \$1,012$
$3 \times \$78 = \$234$
$\$1,012 + \$234 = \$1,246$
He spent **\$1,246** altogether.

$$
\begin{array}{r}
\overset{2}{2}\overset{1}{5}3 \\
\times \quad 4 \\
\hline
1,012
\end{array}
$$

$$
\begin{array}{r}
\overset{2}{7}8 \\
\times \quad 3 \\
\hline
234
\end{array}
$$

53.

	$276			
Bag				} ?
Dresses				

$\$276 \div 4 = \$69$
$7 \times \$69 = \$483$
Anna spends **\$483** on the bag and 3 dresses.

$$
\begin{array}{r}
69 \\
4\overline{)276} \\
24 \\
\hline
36 \\
36 \\
\hline
0
\end{array}
$$

$$
\begin{array}{r}
\overset{6}{6}9 \\
\times \quad 7 \\
\hline
483
\end{array}
$$

54.

| 35 | 35 | 35 | 35 | 219 |

$4 \times 35 = 140$
$140 + 219 = 359$
Jason had **359** marbles to begin with.

$$
\begin{array}{r}
\overset{2}{3}5 \\
\times \quad 4 \\
\hline
140
\end{array}
$$

55.

| 114 | 686 |

$114 + 686 = 800$
$800 \times \$17 = \$13,600$
\$13,600 was collected in all.

$$
\begin{array}{r}
800 \\
\times \quad 17 \\
\hline
5600 \\
800 \\
\hline
13,600
\end{array}
$$

56.

| 840 | 840 | 840 | 840 | 840 | 840 | 840 |

$7 \times 840 = 5,880$
He bakes 5,880 loaves of bread in a week.

$$
\begin{array}{r}
\overset{2}{8}40 \\
\times \quad 7 \\
\hline
5,880
\end{array}
$$

| 5880 | 5880 | 5880 | 5880 | 5880 | 5880 |

$6 \times 5,880 = 35,280$
He will bake **35,280** loaves of bread in 6 weeks.

$$
\begin{array}{r}
\overset{5}{5},\overset{4}{8}80 \\
\times \quad 6 \\
\hline
35,280
\end{array}
$$

57.

| 50 | 50 | 50 | 50 | 50 | 50 | 50 | ? | ? | ? |

$7 \times 50 = 350$
$896 - 350 = 546$
$546 \div 3 = 182$
There are **182** stickers in each album.

$$
\begin{array}{r}
182 \\
3\overline{)546} \\
3 \\
\hline
24 \\
24 \\
\hline
6 \\
6 \\
\hline
0
\end{array}
$$

58. (a) $25 \times 400 = 10,000$
The principal bought **10,000** pieces of candy altogether.

(b) $2,000 \times 7 = 14,000$
$14,000 - 10,000 = 4,000$
$4,000 \div 400 = 40 \div 4 = 10$

$$
\begin{array}{r}
400 \\
\times \quad 25 \\
\hline
2000 \\
800 \\
\hline
10,000
\end{array}
$$

If each child was given 7 pieces, **10** more packages of candy were needed.

59. Use 'Guess and Check' method.

Guess	Her mother's age	Kimi's age	Is her mother 5 times as old as Helen?
1	$44 - 4 = 40$	$16 - 4 = 12$	$40 \div 12 = 3\,R\,4$
2	$44 - 8 = 36$	$16 - 8 = 8$	$36 \div 8 = 4\,R\,4$
3	$44 - 9 = 35$	$16 - 9 = 7$	$35 \div 7 = 5$

Kimi's mother was five times as old as Helen **9** years ago.

60.

$5 \times \$328 = \$1,640$
$\$1,640 \div 8 = \$205$

$$
\begin{array}{r}
\overset{1}{3}\overset{4}{2}8 \\
\times \quad 5 \\
\hline
1,640
\end{array}
$$

$$
\begin{array}{r}
205 \\
8\overline{)1,640} \\
16 \\
\hline
4 \\
0 \\
\hline
40 \\
40 \\
\hline
0
\end{array}
$$

He must pay **\$205** for them each month.

61.

	$3600		
Michael			$320	} ?
Cynthia				

$\$3,600 - \$320 = \$3,280$

$\$3,280 \div 2 = \$1,640$
Cynthia had \$1,640.

$\$3,600 + \$1,640 = \$5,240$
The total amount of money they had was **\$5,240** in the beginning.

$$
\begin{array}{r}
1,640 \\
2\overline{)3,280} \\
2 \\
\hline
12 \\
12 \\
\hline
8 \\
8 \\
\hline
0 \\
0 \\
\hline
0
\end{array}
$$

62.

		$12			
Luis	B	P	P	P	P
Carlos	B	P	P	$4	

$\$4 \div 2 = \$2$
Each pen cost \$2.
$\$12 - (4 \times \$2) = \$4$
The cost of the book was **\$4**.

63. $250 \times \$12 = \$3,000$
\$3,000 was collected from the sale of all the adult tickets.
$\$6,915 - \$3,000 = \$3,915$
$\$3,915 \div \$9 = 435$
435 children went to the zoo.

$$
\begin{array}{r}
\overset{1}{2}50 \\
\times \quad 12 \\
\hline
500 \\
250 \\
\hline
3,000
\end{array}
$$

$$
\begin{array}{r}
435 \\
9\overline{)3,915} \\
36 \\
\hline
31 \\
27 \\
\hline
45 \\
45 \\
\hline
0
\end{array}
$$

64. $\$1,350 - \$400 = \$950$
Each of his six children received \$950.
$\$2,000 + (6 \times \$950) + \$1,350$
$= \$2,000 + \$5,700 + \$1,350$
$= \$9,050$
His bonus was **\$9,050**.

$$
\begin{array}{r}
\overset{3}{9}50 \\
\times \quad 6 \\
\hline
5,700
\end{array}
$$

Unit 4: Line Graphs and Tables

1. **11 birds**
$30 - 8 - 3 - 8 = 11$

2. **birds**
Mario saw 11 birds in the park.

3. **cats**
Mario saw 3 cats in the park.

4. **3 more birds**
   $11 - 8 = 3$
5. **18 animals**
   $3 + 5 + 4 = 12$
   $30 - 12 = 18$
6.

Months	Number of mobile phones sold
November	65
December	30
January	75
February	50
March	40

7. **January**
   He sold 75 mobile phones in January.
8. **20 more mobile phones**
   $50 - 30 = 20$
9. **140 mobile phones**
   $75 + 65 = 140$
10. **80 mobile phones**
    $40 \times 2 = 80$
11. **$9,180**
    $50 + 40 = 90$
    $90 \times \$102 = \$9,180$
12. **150 students**
13. **2006**
    250 students took the school bus in 2006.
14. **100 students**
    $225 - 125 = 100$
15. **125 students**
    $250 - 125 = 125$
16. **750 students**
    $250 + 150 + 125 + 225 = 750$
17.

Name	Amount of money collected
Mandy	**$270**
Kim	**$140**
Felix	**$260**
Ratana	**$200**
Robert	**$130**
Janice	**$140**

18. **Mandy** and **Felix**
    Mandy collected $270 and Felix collected $260.
19. **Kim** and **Janice**
    Both collected $140.
20. **Felix**
    $\$130 \times 2 = \$260$
21. **$1,140**
    $\$270 + \$140 + \$260 + \$200 + \$130 + \$140 = \$1,140$
22. **$860**
    $\$2,000 - \$1,140 = \$860$
23. **3rd week**
    There were 500 visitors in the 3rd week.
24. **2,250 visitors**
    $2,750 - 500 = 2,250$
25. **1,750 visitors**
    $3,500 - 1,750 = 1,750$
26. **3,000 visitors**
    $3,500 - 500 = 3,000$
27. **$76,500**
    $3,500 + 1,750 + 500 + 2,750 = 8,500$
    $8,500 \times \$9 = \$76,500$

Review 2

1. **(4)**

$$
\begin{array}{r}
9\,4\,3 \\
\times\quad 5\,7 \\
\hline
6\,6\,0\,1 \\
4\,7\,1\,5 \\
\hline
5\,3,7\,5\,1
\end{array}
$$

2. **(4)**

$$
\begin{array}{r}
7\,2\,5 \\
10\,\overline{)\,7,2\,5\,6} \\
7\,0 \\
\hline
2\,5 \\
2\,0 \\
\hline
5\,6 \\
5\,0 \\
\hline
6
\end{array}
$$

3. **(2)**
   $140 + 142 + 136 = 418$
   $557 - 418 = 139$ cm
4. **(2)**
   $139 - 136 = 3$ cm
5. **(3)**
   Felicia's test score in mathematics in March was 55.
6. **(2)**
   $80 - 70 = 10$
7. **(1)**
   Felicia scored 80 in mathematics in February.
8. **416**
   $\square \div 8 = 52$
   $\square = 52 \times 8 = 416$
9. **5,400**
   $1,785 \times 3 \approx 1,800 \times 3 = 5,400$
10. **1,530 R 3**

$$
\begin{array}{r}
1,5\,3\,0 \\
4\,\overline{)\,6,1\,2\,3} \\
4 \\
\hline
2\,1 \\
2\,0 \\
\hline
1\,2 \\
1\,2 \\
\hline
3 \\
0 \\
\hline
3
\end{array}
$$

11. **250 Indonesian stamps**
    $394 + 125 + 178 = 697$
    $947 - 697 = 250$
12. **629 coins**
    $127 + 245 + 169 + 88 = 629$
13. **318 more stamps**
    $947 - 629 = 318$
14. **17,015**

$$
\begin{array}{r}
2\,0\,5 \\
\times\quad 8\,3 \\
\hline
6\,1\,5 \\
1\,6\,4\,0 \\
\hline
1\,7,0\,1\,5
\end{array}
$$

15. **989**

$$
\begin{array}{r}
9\,8\,9 \\
8\,\overline{)\,7,9\,1\,6} \\
7\,2 \\
\hline
7\,1 \\
6\,4 \\
\hline
7\,6 \\
7\,2 \\
\hline
4
\end{array}
$$

16.

| Bigger box | 120 |
| Smaller box | ? |

(bracket) 900

$900 - 120 = 780$
$780 \div 2 = 390$
There were **390** pens in the smaller box.

17. $36 \times \$159 = \$5,724$
    $\$8,000 - \$5,724 = \$2,276$
    He earned **$2,276**.

Singapore Math Practice Level 4A

18.

1,230 ÷ 6 = 205
205 × 9 = 1,845
The three children have **1,845** beads altogether.

19. 3,000 − 54 = 2,946
2,946 × $9 = $26,514
The publisher made **$26,514** from the sale of the books.

20. (a)

?							
1,395	1,395	1,395	1,395	1,395	1,395	1,395	1,395

8 × 1,395 = 11,160
The factory can make **11,160** remote-controlled cars in eight weeks.

(b)

40,455

?	?	?	?	?	?	?	?	?

40,455 ÷ 9 = 4,495
The factory must make **4,495** remote-controlled cars in a week.

Unit 5: Fractions

1. $3\frac{1}{2}$
2. $6\frac{2}{3}$
3. $5\frac{1}{4}$
4. $9\frac{1}{12}$
5. $7\frac{5}{7}$
6. $4\frac{5}{8}$
7. $1\frac{4}{9}$
8. $2\frac{3}{5}$
9. $8\frac{1}{6}$
10. $3\frac{9}{11}$
11. $2, 3, 2\frac{3}{5}$
12. $4, 6, 4\frac{6}{7}$
13. $8, 3, 8\frac{3}{8}$
14. $3, 1, 3\frac{1}{6}$
15. $6, 7, 6\frac{7}{12}$
16. $2\frac{3}{5}, 3\frac{2}{5}, 4\frac{4}{5}$
17. $1\frac{3}{9} / 1\frac{1}{3}, 1\frac{8}{9}, 2\frac{7}{9}$
18. $6\frac{4}{7}, 7\frac{1}{7}, 7\frac{4}{7}$
19. **4**
1 whole = 2 halves
2 × 2 = 4
20. **10**
1 whole = 3 thirds
(3 × 3) + 1 = 10
21. **62**

22. **21**
1 whole = 11 elevenths
(5 × 11) + 7 = 62
1 whole = 12 twelfths
(1 × 12) + 9 = 21
23. **61**
1 whole = 7 sevenths
(8 × 7) + 5 = 61
24. **19**
1 whole = 4 quarters
$4\frac{3}{4}$ = (4 × 4) + 3 = 19
25. **11**
1 whole = 6 sixths
(1 × 6) + 5 = 11
26. **75**
1 whole = 8 eighths
(9 × 8) + 3 = 75
27. **67**
1 whole = 10 tenths
(6 × 10) + 7 = 67
28. $\frac{1}{2}, \frac{5}{4}, \frac{9}{4}$
29. $\frac{4}{7}, 1, \frac{9}{7}$
30. $\frac{1}{5}, \frac{6}{5}, 2$
31. $1\frac{1}{2} = \frac{2}{2} + \frac{1}{2} = \frac{\mathbf{3}}{\mathbf{2}}$
32. $1\frac{3}{10} = \frac{10}{10} + \frac{3}{10} = \frac{\mathbf{13}}{\mathbf{10}}$
33. $2\frac{3}{4} = \frac{8}{4} + \frac{3}{4} = \frac{\mathbf{11}}{\mathbf{4}}$
34. $4\frac{3}{5} = \frac{20}{5} + \frac{3}{5} = \frac{\mathbf{23}}{\mathbf{5}}$
35. $7\frac{1}{6} = \frac{42}{6} + \frac{1}{6} = \frac{\mathbf{43}}{\mathbf{6}}$
36. $8\frac{2}{3} = \frac{24}{3} + \frac{2}{3} = \frac{\mathbf{26}}{\mathbf{3}}$
37. $3\frac{5}{8} = \frac{24}{8} + \frac{5}{8} = \frac{\mathbf{29}}{\mathbf{8}}$
38. $3\frac{7}{12} = \frac{36}{12} + \frac{7}{12} = \frac{\mathbf{43}}{\mathbf{12}}$
39. $8\frac{4}{9} = \frac{72}{9} + \frac{4}{9} = \frac{\mathbf{76}}{\mathbf{9}}$
40. $2\frac{4}{7} = \frac{14}{7} + \frac{4}{7} = \frac{\mathbf{18}}{\mathbf{7}}$
41. $\frac{11}{2} = \frac{10}{2} + \frac{1}{2} = 5 + \frac{1}{2} = \mathbf{5\frac{1}{2}}$
42. $\frac{9}{4} = \frac{8}{4} + \frac{1}{4} = 2 + \frac{1}{4} = \mathbf{2\frac{1}{4}}$
43. $\frac{5}{5} = \mathbf{1}$
44. $\frac{16}{2} = \mathbf{8}$
45. $\frac{37}{5} = \frac{35}{5} + \frac{2}{5} = 7 + \frac{2}{5} = \mathbf{7\frac{2}{5}}$
46. $\frac{12}{3} = \mathbf{4}$
47. $\frac{15}{8} = \frac{8}{8} + \frac{7}{8} = 1 + \frac{7}{8} = \mathbf{1\frac{7}{8}}$
48. $\frac{17}{6} = \frac{12}{6} + \frac{5}{6} = 2 + \frac{5}{6} = \mathbf{2\frac{5}{6}}$

49. $\frac{23}{6} = \frac{18}{6} + \frac{5}{6} = 3 + \frac{5}{6} = \mathbf{3\frac{5}{6}}$

50. $\frac{38}{9} = \frac{36}{9} + \frac{2}{9} = 4 + \frac{2}{9} = \mathbf{4\frac{2}{9}}$

51. $\frac{2}{5} + \frac{4}{5} = \frac{6}{5} = \mathbf{1\frac{1}{5}}$

52. $\frac{2}{3} + \frac{4}{9} = \frac{6}{9} + \frac{4}{9} = \frac{10}{9} = \mathbf{1\frac{1}{9}}$

53. $\frac{3}{7} + \frac{13}{14} = \frac{6}{14} + \frac{13}{14} = \frac{19}{14} = \mathbf{1\frac{5}{14}}$

54. $\frac{5}{8} + \frac{3}{4} = \frac{5}{8} + \frac{6}{8} = \frac{11}{8} = \mathbf{1\frac{3}{8}}$

55. $\frac{7}{12} + \frac{2}{6} + \frac{9}{12} = \frac{7}{12} + \frac{4}{12} + \frac{9}{12} = \frac{20}{12} = \mathbf{1\frac{2}{3}}$

56. $\frac{1}{2} + \frac{3}{10} + \frac{9}{10} = \frac{5}{10} + \frac{3}{10} + \frac{9}{10} = \frac{17}{10} = \mathbf{1\frac{7}{10}}$

57. $\frac{2}{4} + \frac{7}{8} + \frac{1}{4} = \frac{4}{8} + \frac{7}{8} + \frac{2}{8} = \frac{13}{8} = \mathbf{1\frac{5}{8}}$

58. $\frac{1}{3} + \frac{3}{9} + \frac{5}{9} = \frac{3}{9} + \frac{3}{9} + \frac{5}{9} = \frac{11}{9} = \mathbf{1\frac{2}{9}}$

59. $6 - \frac{2}{8} = \frac{48}{8} - \frac{2}{8} = \frac{46}{8} = 5\frac{6}{8} = \mathbf{5\frac{3}{4}}$

60. $10 - \frac{5}{12} = \frac{120}{12} - \frac{5}{12} = \frac{115}{12} = \mathbf{9\frac{7}{12}}$

61. $\frac{8}{9} - \frac{2}{9} = \frac{6}{9} = \mathbf{\frac{2}{3}}$

62. $\frac{9}{10} - \frac{1}{2} = \frac{9}{10} - \frac{5}{10} = \frac{4}{10} = \mathbf{\frac{2}{5}}$

63. $2\frac{6}{9} - \frac{1}{3} = 2\frac{6}{9} - \frac{3}{9} = 2\frac{3}{9} = \mathbf{2\frac{1}{3}}$

64. $4\frac{9}{12} - \frac{2}{4} = 4\frac{9}{12} - \frac{6}{12} = 4\frac{3}{12} = \mathbf{4\frac{1}{4}}$

65. $5\frac{7}{12} - \frac{1}{4} = 5\frac{7}{12} - \frac{3}{12} = 5\frac{4}{12} = \mathbf{5\frac{1}{3}}$

66. $7 - \frac{9}{10} - \frac{2}{5} = \frac{70}{10} - \frac{9}{10} - \frac{4}{10} = \frac{57}{10} = \mathbf{5\frac{7}{10}}$

67. $\frac{2}{\cancel{3}_1} \times \cancel{21}^{7} = \mathbf{14}$

68. $\frac{1}{\cancel{8}_1} \times \cancel{72}^{9} = \mathbf{9}$

69. $\frac{5}{\cancel{9}_1} \times \cancel{81}^{9} = \mathbf{45}$

70. $\frac{4}{\cancel{5}_1} \times \cancel{65}^{13} = \mathbf{52}$

71. $\frac{9}{\cancel{10}_1} \times \cancel{20}^{2} = \mathbf{18}$

72. $\frac{5}{\cancel{6}_1} \times \cancel{48}^{8} = \mathbf{40}$

73. $\frac{3}{\cancel{7}_1} \times \cancel{63}^{9} = \mathbf{27}$

74. $\frac{3}{\cancel{4}_1} \times \cancel{52}^{13} = \mathbf{39}$

75. $\frac{4}{\cancel{9}_1} \times \cancel{27}^{3} = \mathbf{12}$

76. $\frac{1}{\cancel{6}_1} \times \cancel{84}^{14} = \mathbf{14}$

77. $1 - \frac{3}{8} = \frac{8}{8} - \frac{3}{8} = \frac{5}{8}$

She had $\frac{5}{8}$ of the cake left.

78. $\frac{7}{12} - \frac{1}{6} = \frac{7}{12} - \frac{2}{12} = \frac{5}{12}$

The mass of the sand in the can is $\frac{5}{12}$ lb.

79. $\frac{5}{6} + \frac{1}{10} + \frac{9}{10} = \frac{50}{60} + \frac{6}{60} + \frac{54}{60}$

$= \frac{110}{60} = 1\frac{50}{60} = 1\frac{5}{6}$

The total mass of the three boxes is $1\frac{5}{6}$ kg.

80. $\frac{1}{4} + \frac{5}{12} = \frac{3}{12} + \frac{5}{12} = \frac{8}{12}$

$\frac{11}{12} - \frac{8}{12} = \frac{3}{12} = \frac{1}{4}$

The length of ribbon Mrs. Kwan cut was $\frac{1}{4}$ m.

81. $\frac{1}{3} + \frac{5}{9} = \frac{3}{9} + \frac{5}{9} = \frac{8}{9}$

$1\frac{2}{3} - \frac{8}{9} = \frac{5}{3} - \frac{8}{9} = \frac{15}{9} - \frac{8}{9} = \frac{7}{9}$

Lina prepared $\frac{7}{9}$ L of fruit punch.

82. $\frac{6}{10} - \frac{1}{2} = \frac{6}{10} - \frac{5}{10} = \frac{1}{10}$

$\frac{6}{10} + \frac{1}{10} = \frac{7}{10}$

The two children drank $\frac{7}{10}$ L of milk in all.

83. $\frac{1}{4} + \frac{1}{8} = \frac{2}{8} + \frac{1}{8} = \frac{3}{8}$

$5 - \frac{3}{8} = \frac{40}{8} - \frac{3}{8} = \frac{37}{8} = 4\frac{5}{8}$

She had $\mathbf{4\frac{5}{8}}$ L of cooking oil left.

84. $\frac{3}{4} + \frac{3}{8} = \frac{6}{8} + \frac{3}{8} = \frac{9}{8}$

$12\frac{7}{8} - \frac{9}{8} = 12\frac{7}{8} - 1\frac{1}{8} = 11\frac{6}{8} = 11\frac{3}{4}$

She cycled $\mathbf{11\frac{3}{4}}$ km.

85. $16 + 24 + 20 = 60$

There are 60 beads in a box.

$\frac{20}{60} = \frac{1}{3}$

$\frac{1}{3}$ of the beads in the box are blue.

86.
18 mi.

$\frac{1}{\cancel{6}_1} \times \cancel{18}^{3} = 3$ mi.

$3 \times 5 = 15$ mi.

He has to travel **15 miles** in order to reach Town B.

87.

$32 \div 8 = 4$
$3 \times 4 = 12$
Tara ate **12** chocolates.

88.

108

Singapore Math Practice Level 4A

(a) 28 + 15 + 7 = 50
Farmer Bill had 50 birds.
50 ÷ 5 = 10
4 × 10 = 40
He sold **40** birds in all.

(b) 28 − 12 = 16
He had 16 chickens left.
$\frac{16}{28} = \frac{4}{7}$
$\frac{4}{7}$ of the chickens were left.

89. $1 - \frac{5}{8} - \frac{1}{4} = \frac{8}{8} - \frac{5}{8} - \frac{2}{8} = \frac{1}{8}$

$\frac{1}{\cancel{8}} \times \cancel{568}^{71} = 71$

There were **71** children at the concert.

90. $\frac{2}{3} \rightarrow \$60$

$\frac{1}{3} \rightarrow \$60 \div 2 = \$30$

$3 \times \$30 = \$90$

Isabel received **\$90**.

Unit 6: Angles

1. ∠ABC = ∠**y**
∠ACB = ∠**x**
∠BAC = ∠**z**

2. ∠d = ∠**SRQ** / ∠**QRS**
∠e = ∠**OSR** / ∠**RSO**
∠f = ∠**SOP** / ∠**POS**
∠g = ∠**OPQ** / ∠**QPO**
∠h = ∠**PQR** / ∠**RQP**

3. ∠**b**, ∠**c**, ∠**d**, ∠**f**

4. ∠**a**, ∠**e**

Estimated value	Actual measurement
5. ∠a = **100°**	∠a = **98°**
6. ∠b = **70°**	∠b = **62°**
7. ∠PQR = **100°**	∠PQR = **105°**
8. ∠XWY = **120°**	∠XWY = **126°**

9.

10.

11.

12.

13. $\frac{1}{4}$ / quarter
14. **180**
15. $\frac{3}{4}$ / **three-quarter**
16. **4**
17. $\frac{1}{2}$ / **Half**
18. $\frac{1}{4}$ / **Quarter**
19. Tony: **north**
Aaron: **northeast**
Susan: **east**
Jasmin: **southeast**
Maggie: **south**
Sam: **southwest**
Malik: **west**
Zack: **northwest**
20. (a) **northwest**
(b) **southeast**
(c) **west**
(d) **east**
(e) **north**
(f) **east**
(g) **northeast**
(h) **southwest**
21. (a) **225**
(b) **180**
(c) **270**
(d) **45**
(e) $\frac{1}{4}$ / **quarter**
(f) $\frac{3}{4}$ / **three-quarter**

Review 3

1. **(3)**
$6\frac{7}{9} = \frac{54}{9} + \frac{7}{9} = \frac{61}{9}$

2. **(4)**
$\frac{2}{5} - \frac{3}{10} = \frac{4}{10} - \frac{3}{10} = \frac{1}{10}$

3. **(4)**
$\frac{4}{9} + \frac{2}{3} = \frac{4}{9} + \frac{6}{9} = \frac{10}{9} = \frac{9}{9} + \frac{1}{9} = 1\frac{1}{9}$

4. **(4)**
$\frac{\text{Shaded triangles}}{\text{Total triangles}} = \frac{7}{12}$

5. **(1)**
$\frac{2}{\cancel{7}} \times \cancel{98}^{14} = 28$

6. **(3)**
1 whole = 6 sixths
(5 × 6) + 1 = 31

7. **(3)**
∠a = 18°

8. $32\frac{2}{6} = \mathbf{32\frac{1}{3}}$

9. $\frac{24}{5} = \frac{20}{5} + \frac{4}{5} = \mathbf{4\frac{4}{5}}$

10. $\frac{3}{4}$ / Three-quarter

11. $1 - \frac{1}{2} - \frac{3}{8} = \frac{8}{8} - \frac{4}{8} - \frac{3}{8} = \frac{1}{8}$

12. **∠XZY / ∠YZX**

13. $\frac{3}{4} \times 25 = \frac{75}{4} = \mathbf{18 \frac{3}{4} L}$

14. **Andy**

15. **135°**

16.

32 – 8 = 24
24 ÷ 2 = 12
There were 12 girls.

$\frac{8}{12} = \frac{2}{3}$

$\frac{2}{3}$ of the girls wore glasses at the party.

17. $\frac{3}{8} \times 104 = 39$
There were 39 women.

104 – 39 – 28 = 37
There were **37** men.

18. $\frac{4}{7} \rightarrow \$96$

$\frac{1}{7} \rightarrow \$96 \div 4 = \$24$

$\frac{4}{7} + \frac{2}{7} = \frac{6}{7}$

$\frac{6}{7} \rightarrow 6 \times \$24 = \$144$

She spent **$144** in all.

19.

20. (a) **southeast / SE**
    (b) **north / N**
    (c) **northeast / NE**
    (d) **northwest / NW**
    (e) **west / W**

Unit 7: Perpendicular and Parallel Lines

1.

2.

3. (a) & (b)

4. (a) & (b)

5.

6.

7. (a) & (b)

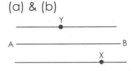

8. (a) **JB // HC, JB // GD, JB // FE, HC // GD,**
       HC // FE, GD // FE, AK // CL
   (b) **AK ⊥ JB, AK ⊥ HC, AK ⊥ GD, AK ⊥ FE,**
       CL ⊥ GD, CL ⊥ FE, LC ⊥ HC

9. (a) & (b)

10. (a) **AB, GH, EF, DC**
    (b) **EA, DG, FB, CH**

11. (a) **vertical**
    (b) **horizontal**
    (c) **vertical**
    (d) **horizontal**

Unit 8: Rectangles and Squares

1. (a) **rectangle**
   (b) **It has four sides. / It has two pairs of parallel lines. /**
       All four angles are right angles. / Its opposite sides
       are equal.

2. (a) **rectangle**
   (b) **It has four sides. / It has two pairs of parallel lines. /**
       All four angles are right angles. / Its opposite sides
       are equal.

3. (a) **square**
   (b) **It has four sides. / All four sides are equal. / It has**
       two pairs of parallel lines. / All four angles are right
       angles.

4.

5.

6. x = **12**
   y = **5**
7. x = 40 ÷ 5 = **8**
   y = **40**
8. x = **10**
   y = **10**
9. 90° − 15° = **75°**
10. 90° − 25° − 18° = **47°**
11. 90° − 62° − 8° = **20°**
12. 90° − 67° − 10° = **13°**
13. 90° − 31° − 13° = **46°**
14. AB = 5 + 8 + 5 = **18 in.**
    AH = **8 in.**
    AH has the same length as BC.
15. DF = 10 + 10 + 15 = **35 cm**
    EF = 10 + 15 = **25 cm**
16. EF = 32 − 11 − 4 = **17 ft.**
    DE = 21 − 8 − 5 = **8 ft.**
17. ML = (16 + 8) − 16 = **8 cm**
    AB = 16 + 8 + 8 = **32 cm**
18. BC = 18 − 8 − 6 = **4 in.**
    EF = 33 − 15 = **18 in.**

Review 4
1. **(1)**
2. **(2)**

3. **(1)**
   17 − 3 = 14 cm
4. **(1)**
   90° − 26° − 48° = 16°
5. **(3)**
   48 ÷ 2 = 24 cm
6. **(3)**
   24 − 13 = 11 cm
7. **(2)**
8. **(3)**
9. **(1)**

10. **(2)**
    There are 3 horizontal lines in the figure.
11. **EF**
12. **36°**
    90° − 18° = 72°
    72° ÷ 2 = 36°
13. **It has four sides. / All four sides are equal. / It has two pairs of parallel lines. / All four angles are right angles.**

14. **25 in.**
    108 − 83 = 25 in.
15. **AH // DE** and **AH // FG**
16. (a) **parallel / vertical**
    (b) **parallel / horizontal**
17. (a) **horizontal**
    (b) **vertical**
18. **BC**
19.

20. Accept other correct answers.

Final Review
1. **(4)**
   1,500 + 86,576 = 88,076
2. **(3)**
   The number 0 is in the hundreds place.
3. **(2)**
4. **(3)**
   2 × 33 = 66
   3 × 22 = 66
   6 × 11 = 66
5. **(3)**
   9,004 ≈ 9,000
6. **(4)**
   $3\frac{2}{5} = \frac{15}{5} + \frac{2}{5} = \frac{17}{5}$
7. **(2)**
   $$\begin{array}{r} \overset{7}{3}\,\overset{}{9}\,\overset{3}{0}\,4 \\ \times \qquad 8 \\ \hline 3\,1{,}2\,3\,2 \end{array}$$
8. **(4)**
   1 whole = 4 quarters
   (5 × 4) + 3 = 23
9. **(3)**

   | Thursday | 1,659 | | | |
   | Friday | 1,659 | 1,659 | 1,659 | } ? |

   4 × 1,659 = 6,636
10. **(4)**
    $40 + $10 = $50
    Anya had $50 at first.
    $\frac{40}{50} = \frac{4}{5}$
11. **(4)**
    90 + 81 + 75 = 246
12. **(4)**
    90 − 63 = 27

13. **(2)**

14. **(2)**

15. **(4)**

16. **(2)**

$3 \times 8 = 24$

17. **(2)**

$SR = 15 - 3 = 12$ yd.

$QR = SR = 12$ yd.

18. **(4)**

$14,000 + 58,750 = 72,750$

19. **(3)**

```
        1 8 6
   8 ) 1, 4 8 9
        8
        6 8
        6 4
          4 9
          4 8
            1
```

20. **(1)**

21. **28,164**

$20,000 + 5,000 + 3,100 + 60 + 4 = 28,164$

22. **35,150**

$35,310 - 35,230 = 80$

$35,070 + 80 = 35,150$

23. $\dfrac{1}{2}$ / **half**

24. **19,684**

```
       2 1
       5 3 2
    ×    3 7
     3 7 2 4
   1 5 9 6
   1 9, 6 8 4
```

25. **3** and **7**

The multiples of 3 are 3, 6, 9, 12, 15, 18, ㉑, 24, 27, 30, 33, 36, 39, ㊷, 45, 48, 51, ...

The multiples of 7 are 7, 14, ㉑, 28, 35, ㊷, 49, 56, ...

26. $\dfrac{58}{6} = \dfrac{54}{6} + \dfrac{4}{6} = 9 + \dfrac{4}{6} = 9\dfrac{4}{6} = \mathbf{9\dfrac{2}{3}}$

27. **64°**

28.

29. $\angle a = 90° - 55° - 18° = \mathbf{17°}$

$\angle b = 90° - 28° = \mathbf{62°}$

30. $3 + \dfrac{2}{5} + \dfrac{9}{10} = 3 + \dfrac{4}{10} + \dfrac{9}{10} = 3\dfrac{13}{10} = \mathbf{4\dfrac{3}{10}}$

31.

32.

33.

Day	Number of pots of flowers
Monday	16
Tuesday	12
Wednesday	18
Thursday	20
Friday	24

34. **90**

$16 + 12 + 18 + 20 + 24 = 90$

35. $421 \div 8 \approx 400 \div 8 = \mathbf{50}$

36. **2**

37. **187**

$\square \div 7 = 26$ R 5

$\square = 7 \times 26 + 5 = 187$

38. **2 lb.**

$1 - \dfrac{5}{6} = \dfrac{1}{6}$

$\dfrac{1}{6} \times \overset{2}{\cancel{12}} = 2$

39. $9,055 \times 7 \approx 9,000 \times 7 = \mathbf{63,000}$

40.

270°

41. $8 \times \$630 = \$5,040$

\$5,040

TV	stereo	left
?	\$295	\$1853

$\$295 + \$1,853 = \$2,148$

$\$5,040 - \$2,148 = \$2,892$

The cost of the television set was **\$2,892**.

42.

book | ?

soccer ball | | \$15

car | | \$15 | \$198

\$230

$\$230 - \$198 - \$15 - \$17$

The cost of the book is **\$17**.

43. $\dfrac{1}{4} + \dfrac{1}{8} = \dfrac{2}{8} + \dfrac{1}{8} = \dfrac{3}{8}$

Juan ate $\frac{3}{8}$ of the pizza.

$1 - \frac{1}{4} - \frac{3}{8} = \frac{8}{8} - \frac{2}{8} - \frac{3}{8} = \frac{3}{8}$

Cindy ate $\frac{3}{8}$ of the pizza.

44. $\frac{3}{\underset{1}{8}} \times \overset{7}{\cancel{56}} = 21$

Esther gave 21 stickers to her sister.

$56 - 21 - 18 = 17$

She gave **17** stickers to her friend.

45. Use 'Guess and Check' method.

Guess	Mr. Popovic's age	Granddaughter's age	Is Mr. Popovic 5 times as old as her granddaughter?
1	78	14	No $78 \div 14 = 5 \text{ R } 8$
2	80	16	Yes $80 \div 16 = 5$

Mr. Popovic will be five times as old as his granddaughter in **4** years' time.

Challenge Questions

1.

Day	1	2	3	4	5	6	7	8
No. of eggs sold	15	25	36	48	61	75	90	106

$+10 \quad +11 \quad +12 \quad +13 \quad +14 \quad +15 \quad +16$

2.

Shani
Jenny
Enrique

$57 + 3 = 60$
$60 \div 6 = 10$
$10 + 4 = 14$

Jenny will be **14** years old in four years.

3. Use 'Guess and Check' method.

A	B	A ÷ B	Check
29	5	$5\frac{4}{5}$	✗
29	4	$7\frac{1}{4}$	✗
28	5	$5\frac{3}{5}$	✗
28	4	7	✗
26	4	$6\frac{1}{2}$	✗
25	4	$6\frac{1}{4}$	✓

A is **25** and B is **4**.

4. second digit: $3 \times 3 = 9$
   fourth digit: $2 \times 3 = 6$
   third digit: $9 - 6 = 3$
   first digit: $9 - 2 = 7$
   last digit: $7 - 2 = 5$
   I am **79,365**.

5. Use 'Guess and Check' method.

X	Y	product	sum	
10	40	$10 \times 40 = 400$	$10 + 40 = 50$	
20	30	$20 \times 30 = 600$	$20 + 30 = 50$	✓

X is **20** and Y is **30**.

6. $6 \times 10 = 60$

Jason's score in the test was 60.

$172 - 60 = 112$
$112 \div 7 = 16$
$6 \times 16 = 96$

Chet's score in the test was **96**.

7. Use 'Guess and Check' method.

Number 1	Number 2	Quotient	Difference	Check
10	120	12	110	✗
11	132	12	121	✗
12	144	12	132	✓

The two numbers are **12** and **144** respectively.

8.

Week	1	2	3	4	5	6	7	8
Savings	$2	$4	$6	$8	$10	$12	$14	$16

$\$2 + \$4 + \$6 + \$8 + \$10 + \$12 + \$14 + \$16 = \$72$
The bag costs **$72**.

9. Factors of 8 are 1, 2, 4, and 8.
   1st × 4th = $4 \times 8 = 32$
   1st digit: 8 (the largest single digit for factors of 8)
   4th digit: 4 ($32 \div 8 = 4$)
   2nd digit: 1 ($4 - 3 = 1$)
   3rd digit: 2
   I am **8,124**.

10. First six multiples of 6 are 6, 12, 18, 24, 30, and 36.
    10th multiple of 6 is 60.
    11th multiple of 6 is 66.

6	30	24	$6 + 30 + 24 = 60$
18	12	36	$18 + 12 + 36 = 66$

11.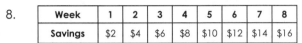

Mr. Garza
Mrs. Garza
Her sister $1255

$7 \times \$1,255 = \$8,785$
$12 \times \$8,785 = \$105,420$
The three of them earn **$105,420** in a year.

12.

$360° \div 12 = 30°$

When the minute hand moves from one number to the other, it turns 30°.

$5 \times 30° = 150°$

The minute hand will point at 5 when turns 150°.

Sylvia eats her breakfast at **8:25 A.M.**

Notes

Notes

Notes

Notes

Notes

Singapore Math Practice Level 4A

Notes

Notes

Singapore Math Practice Level 4A

Notes

Notes

Notes

Notes

Notes

Notes

Singapore Math Practice Level 4A